Christine,
Thank you for all of your help
with our wedding & for making
our delicious wedding cake!
   Love
   Lindsey & Kurtis

island lake lodge ®

island lake lodge
the cookbook

Keith Liggett

photography by Henry Georgi

whitecap

Whitecap Books

Whitecap Books is known for its expertise in the cookbook market, and has produced some of the most innovative and familiar titles found in kitchens across North America. Visit our website at www.whitecap.ca.

Cover and interior design: Mauve Pagé
Photographs: Henry Georgi
Proofreading: Joan E. Templeton

Printed in China

Recipes included by permission of the current and former chefs of Island Lake Lodge: Kelly Attwells, Keith Farkas, Yan Thereian, Alain Stahl, Kerri Maier, Johanne Ratthe, Mark Butcher, and Andy Robidoux.

Library and Archives Canada Cataloguing
in Publication

Liggett, Thomas Keith, 1950–

    Island Lake Lodge : the cookbook / Thomas Keith Liggett.

Includes index.

ISBN 978-1-55285-947-6

    1. Cookery, Canadian—British Columbia style.
2. Island Lake Lodge (B.C.). I. Title.

TX715.6.L544 2009   641.509711'65   C2008-905580-2

The publisher acknowledges the financial support of the Government of Canada through the Book Publishing Industry Development Program (BPIDP) and the Province of British Columbia through the Book Publishing Tax Credit.

09 10 11 12 13   5 4 3 2 1

Contents

The Road to Island Lake Lodge

IN THE WINTER, THE ROAD TO ISLAND LAKE LODGE begins and ends in a steep-walled white pit of a parking lot two klicks off the "Powder Highway," as Highway 3 is affectionately known. The walls rise vertically maybe three metres or more. Carved by a massive snow blower, the lot holds a mix of winter-worn 4-wheel drives and suburban SUVs carrying a light patina of highway dirt. Now, at the end of the day, the sun only hits the very summits of the rocky spires that form the ridge. The last light reflects into the valley briefly removing growing pockets of darkness in the surrounding woods.

I step out of my car. It's not too cold. Slinging my boots over one shoulder and carrying my poles and duffel in one hand, I join a small group standing at the uphill side of the lot. I tip my head back and breathe out. My breath rises in a column and slowly dissipates in the still, cold air. No wind. The snow squeaks and feels sticky underfoot.

The rumble of a snowcat emanates from the woods. A pair of lights breaks a dark gap in the trees. A red cat slows, tips forward and drops down a steep ramp toward us. At a crawl, treads barely moving, it spins around in place and halts, facing back toward the ramp.

The diesel stops. The evening is silent again. A steady ticking comes off the cooling engine. The cab opens and a bundled woman steps out. "Hi, I'm Mel, your ride to the Lodge. Let's get loaded." Pulling on her gloves, she hops off and starts loading skis and duffels. We clamber up the slippery tracks into the cabin on the back of the cat.

With everyone loaded, Mel scampers up the track, and pokes her head in the door. "It's about twenty min-utes, maybe half an hour." Closing the door, she moves forward to the driver's cab. The diesel rumbles, catches. With a little lurch and then a harsher jolt, the cat starts across the few flat feet, rises skyward up the ramp and levels out, moving into the surrounding darkened forest.

The ride is punctuated by stories. Of the Lodge. Of other cat skiing operations. Of great skiing. And of more great skiing.

After a bit, the darkness is broken by a glow. I glimpse lights between the trees. The cat swings around a right-hand corner and into a snow-covered meadow holding four massive log cabins lit from within. The closest invites us with a large, peaked portico extending over a broad set of stone steps leading to double doors.

Mel pulls up, opening the cabin door. "Here you are. I'll drop your poles and skis at the Bear." As we disembark, she effortlessly pulls our duffels from the carrier. "Get settled. Dinner's at eight. Back here."

The four cabins of Island Lake Lodge sit in the centre of 7000 acres of private wilderness. In the winter, the only access is by Island Lake Lodge snowcat. The Lodge hosts 36 skiers at a time. Their days spent skiing off the ridges and down the bowls of bottomless powder surrounding the Lodge. Their evenings spent in front of a blazing fire recounting the runs, the falls, the day.

When Dan MacDonald, Island Lake's founder, talks about starting, he shrugs, "I was a carpenter and needed a winter job. Back then everything shut down in the winter."

The idea was deceptively simple—a poor man's heli-ski operation. Snowcats were far cheaper than helicopters and operate in all weather conditions. First, Dan tried securing a provincial tenure, but found jumping through one hoop brought two or three more hoops. On an off chance, he wrote Shell headquarters asking to lease the 7000-acre headwaters of Lizard Creek. A week later, Dan had a deal—signed, sealed, and delivered. He smiles, shaking his head. You can read his mind: *"That was easy."*

That was the fall of 1983.

For the first few years, skiers gathered in the lower parking lot and rode the cats into the basin to ski. In 1986, Dan and his partners built the first lodge, the Bear. With the Bear, a chef was hired, Alain Stahl.

With the opening of the Bear lodge, word quickly spread, fed equally by the exceptional skiing and the innovative dining. These two complementary aspects looped and entwined like a pair of figure-eight tracks.

Warren Miller, Greg Stump, and the ski-movie producers who followed in their footsteps flocked to the isolated alpine valley, which receives 11 metres of snow every winter. In feature film after feature film, the powder, the cliffs, and the rugged scenery of Island Lake Lodge lit the silver screen.

Dan laughs as he remembers long days with film crews in the snow and long nights of beers and shots in front of the fire back at the Lodge. Then he turns serious. "Shell decided to sell. We were given a 30-day window to come up with a ten percent non-refundable deposit." He shakes his head, laughing, "I brought in anyone with a cheque book. Anyone with a hundred grand was my best friend." Customers became investors, following their hearts with their money. In the end, there were 13 major partners.

The board and Dan began to disagree on the direction of the Lodge. In 2000, the board fired Dan as general manager. He stayed on the board and remained an owner. The initial conflict remained, so after eight months he sold his position and moved on.

Four years ago, the Lodge came up for sale. Dan found a new general partner in Patrick Callahan and re-established a minority stake. He smiles again, lifting his hands with the question, "Who would have thought?"

Today Island Lake Lodge embodies the finest traditions of Canadian skiing with the added refinement of an unparalleled dining experience.

On a summer's evening, we drive up the road to Island Lake Lodge. In the summer the Lodge opens to the public, and is a favorite with Fernie locals and visitors alike. The day passed without a cloud in the sky. As the sun drops behind the ridge, a mountain chill draws the heat from the day. Six of us sit on the deck—Christa, Henry, Steve, myself, and Michael and Kristina from Vancouver. There is no breeze. The lake below reflects the changing tones of the valley perfectly.

Michael asks Steve how long he's been with the Lodge.

Steve laughs, looking at Henry, seated at the other end of the table. "Thanks to Henry, 20 years now. The first year I was doing a bit of guiding and cat driving. We were up for a photo shoot. I drove some. I skied some. The next day we were going over to Crowsnest to shoot. At the end of that day, Dan told me I'd be trail guide the next day. I said no, that I was shooting with Henry. I made more money. Dan did a double take and offered me a job. More than I expected. I took it. Been here ever since."

The appetizers arrive. Another bottle of wine. Steve steps into the Lodge and returns with a pair of binoculars. Scanning the ridges, he spots a herd of goats high on Big White. Having moved the north side to escape the heat, they are about to crest the ridge. He hands the glasses to Michael and tries to point the goats out.

We talk about the spirit of the Lodge in the winter. Skiing. The bond from skiing with the same group for days at a time. How some groups return for the same week, year after year. How each week becomes a family reunion of sorts.

Michael looks at the four locals around the table. "You're all here for the skiing?"

We look at each other in the fading light. Shrug our shoulders. Some say, "Yes." Some simply nod.

Island Lake Lodge embodies a chosen life in the mountains—the skiing and the food. A life of following passion.

Enjoy.

—Keith Liggett

The Details

THERE IS A ZEN STORY OF A MASTER WHO WALKS into an almost finished zendo and asks one of the monks working on the building, "How are we doing?"

The monk replies, "Only a few little details to finish."

The master whacks the monk, exclaiming, "They're *all* details!"

To the chefs of Island Lake Lodge, they're all details. That's how the food maintains its constant high quality. In preparing these dishes at home, remember the same. The difference between organic, locally grown and mass-produced ingredients is subtle, but substantial. Free-range chicken tastes different from factory-raised chicken. Little dashes of flavour lift the dishes out of the ordinary. The pinch of salt to taste may be the pinch that puts the dish over the top.

A pinch of salt. A dash of coriander. And the big details establish a solid foundation for the dish. Bring home the organic and free-range meats instead of factory-raised meats, for a start.

Some recipes may seem complicated and daunting, but once you begin the process they are actually simple and logical. And worthwhile.

Bon appetit.

Breakfast & Brunch

Three Bears Baked Oatmeal

2 eggs
3 cups old-fashioned
    rolled oats

1 cup packed brown sugar
1 cup butter, softened
1 cup milk

1 tsp baking powder
½ tsp salt

Looking out at the peaks of the Three Bears from the Lodge, you will feel a little like Goldilocks eating this homemade oatmeal. For a heartier version, add your favourite fresh or dried fruit and unsalted nuts. Or try it with a little maple syrup and cream. SERVES 4–6

In a shallow 8-cup ovenproof dish, beat eggs lightly. Stir in oats, brown sugar, butter, milk, baking powder, and salt until well combined. Refrigerate, covered, for at least 8 hours or overnight.

One hour before serving, preheat the oven to 350°F. Bake oatmeal, covered, for 45–50 minutes or until firm to the touch.

Star Anise French Toast

6 eggs
1 cup milk
1 Tbsp granulated sugar
2 whole star anise

Pinch salt
6 slices stale bread
Softened butter or canola oil
  for frying

Maple syrup and icing sugar
  to serve
Whole star anise for garnish

In France, French toast is called pain perdu, *or "lost bread," and it's a good use for stale bread. In fact, the drier the bread, the more egg it absorbs and the moister the French toast. If you don't have star anise, substitute 1 teaspoon cinnamon, in which case you don't need to infuse the egg mixture overnight but can use it immediately.* **SERVES 4–6**

In a shallow bowl, whisk together eggs, milk, sugar, star anise, and salt. Refrigerate, covered, for at least 8 hours or overnight for flavours to infuse.

Just before serving, dip bread slices in egg mixture until thoroughly soaked. Heat the butter or oil in a large greased non-stick skillet over medium heat. Cook bread slices, in batches, for about 3 minutes on each side or until golden brown.

Dust with icing sugar and serve with maple syrup. Garnish with the whole star anise.

Johanne Ratthe
PASTRY & MORNING CHEF

OF MID-HEIGHT WITH DARK HAIR SWEEPING her shoulders, Johanne seems little removed from her Quebecois upbringing. Her voice still carries the strong lilting accent, and she occasionally slides by a reversed modifier.

"I started as an apprentice in the CP Hotels. We had our own pastry departments, our own chefs just for pastries. The hotel sent me off for six months to train in pastry. When it was over, I wanted to stay. Not leave. In those six months I discovered what I wanted to do.

"I came to Island Lake Lodge through Yan. We worked together at the Kananaskis Hotel. He left to work at the Lodge. A year later, when he took over the kitchen at the Lodge, he tried to get me to move down to Fernie. I decided not to. In March or April of the year after, we met again during a competition in Calgary."

Johanne repeats their conversation: "'You want to work for me at the Lodge?'—'Oh, I don't know.' 'Let's meet for beers.'

"And that was it.

"I only work at the Lodge in the winters and I lead hiking tours in the summers. The Lodge provides so much freedom for a chef. You can do anything you want.

"Most kitchens are caves with no windows. The Lodge kitchen must have the best view in the world. Everyone comes to work with a smile on his or her face.

"At the end of the day, I walk out the back door with crumbs and the whiskey jacks come right up looking for their handout."

She smiles. "Such a great place. So much snow. And the people."

She smiles again.

Gingerbread Pancakes

1½ cups all-purpose flour
1 cup packed brown sugar
1 tsp baking powder
1 tsp baking soda
1 tsp cinnamon
1 tsp ground ginger

Pinch grated nutmeg
Pinch salt
1 cup cold black coffee
1 cup canola oil
⅔ cup water
2 eggs

2 Tbsp fresh lemon juice
Additional canola oil for frying
Maple syrup and icing sugar
    to serve

These dairy-free pancakes are the perfect morning treat for lactose-intolerant guests. **SERVES 4–6**

In a large bowl, whisk together flour, sugar, baking powder, baking soda, cinnamon, ginger, nutmeg, and salt until well combined. In a medium bowl, whisk together coffee, canola oil, water, eggs, and lemon juice until smooth. Gradually add coffee mixture to flour mixture, stirring until almost smooth.

Heat a large oiled non-stick skillet over medium heat. Pour about ¼ cup batter for each pancake into skillet. Cook for about 2 minutes or until golden brown on undersides. Flip pancakes, then cook for about 1 minute until golden. Remove pancakes from skillet and keep warm. Repeat with remaining batter, oiling skillet occasionally if necessary.

Dust with icing sugar and serve with maple syrup.

Orange and Cranberry Waffles

2 cups all-purpose flour
1 Tbsp baking powder
Pinch salt
4 eggs, separated
1¼ cups milk

½ cup frozen orange juice
  concentrate, thawed
¼ cup canola oil
2 Tbsp dried cranberries
Grated zest of 1 orange

Additional canola oil
  for greasing
Maple syrup to serve

The sweet and tart flavour of these waffles makes them a welcome wake-up dish. SERVES 4–6

In a medium bowl, whisk together flour, baking power, and salt until well combined. In a large bowl, whisk together egg yolks, milk, orange juice concentrate, and oil until smooth.

In a separate medium bowl and using clean beaters, beat egg whites until they hold stiff peaks.

Stir flour mixture into egg yolk mixture until well combined. Stir in cranberries and orange zest. Stir in one-quarter of egg whites to lighten batter, then fold in remaining egg whites until no white streaks remain.

Heat a waffle iron, then brush lightly with a little oil. Pour about ½ cup batter into waffle iron. Close lid. Cook for 4–5 minutes or until steam stops coming out of the waffle iron and waffle is crisp and golden. Remove waffle and keep warm. Repeat with remaining batter, lightly oiling waffle iron before cooking each waffle.

Serve with maple syrup.

Trilogy of Quail Eggs Benedict

ROASTED TOMATOES
6 plum tomatoes
3 Tbsp olive oil
2 tsp coarse salt

EGGS BENEDICT
6 English muffins
5 Tbsp olive oil
Salt and ground black pepper

4 thin slices pancetta
Hollandaise sauce (see Chicken
    Supreme with Tomato
    Hollandaise, page 104; omit
    tomatoes and tomato paste)
3 Tbsp truffle oil
1 Tbsp white vinegar
12 quail eggs
4 thin slices smoked salmon

4 Tbsp crumbled soft
    goat cheese
4 basil leaves
1 cup mesclun mix
1 tsp balsamic vinegar
Finely chopped chives or
    fennel fronds, or edible
    flowers for garnish

A trio of eggs "Benny" variations on each plate—one topped with smoked salmon, another with crisp pancetta, and the third with roasted tomatoes—means no one has to choose. Add quails' eggs and truffled mayo, and a breakfast classic becomes a special-occasion dish. If you can't find quails' eggs, substitute 4 large organic hens' eggs, cook them for 3 to 5 minutes and centre them on the English muffin rounds. **SERVES 4**

ROASTED TOMATOES Preheat the oven to 275°F. Line a large baking sheet with parchment paper. Cut tomatoes into quarters. In a medium bowl, toss tomatoes with olive oil and salt. Spread tomatoes out on prepared baking sheet. Roast for 2 hours or until slightly shrivelled. Set aside to cool to room temperature.

Place tomatoes and their juices in a food processor. Pulse until chopped but still fairly chunky. (Tomatoes may be prepared ahead and refrigerated for up to 24 hours.)

EGGS BENEDICT Preheat the oven to 375°F. Split muffins in half horizontally. Using a 2-inch cookie cutter, cut 12 rounds from muffin halves, discarding trimmings. Brush rounds with 4 Tbsp olive oil, then sprinkle with salt and pepper to taste. Arrange on a baking sheet. Toast in the oven for 8–10 minutes or until golden brown and crisp. Set aside.

Arrange pancetta on baking sheet. Bake for 10–12 minutes or until crisp. Set aside.

Prepare the hollandaise sauce. Stir truffle oil into sauce. Keep warm but do not boil.

Pour water into a wide shallow saucepan to a depth of 2 inches. Bring to a simmer over medium heat, then add vinegar. Carefully break 1 quail egg into a small bowl. Slide egg into simmering water. Repeat with remaining eggs. Poach for 2–3 minutes or until done to taste. Carefully remove eggs with a slotted spoon, then drain on a plate lined with paper towel.

TO SERVE Arrange 3 muffin rounds on each of 4 plates. Top one muffin round on each plate with a slice of pancetta. Top a second muffin round with a slice of smoked salmon and 1 Tbsp goat cheese. Top the remaining muffin rounds with a spoonful of roasted tomato and a basil leaf. Carefully place 1 poached egg on each muffin round. Drizzle each egg with hollandaise. Toss mesclun mix with remaining olive oil, the balsamic vinegar, and salt and pepper to taste. Garnish each plate with mesclun mix, and chives, fennel fronds, or edible flowers.

Soups & Salads

Saffron-Mussel Soup

MUSSELS
4 lb mussels, in their shells
2 Tbsp olive oil
1 onion, finely diced
3 cloves garlic, minced
½ cup dry white wine
2 bay leaves

SOUP
1 cup boiling water
Pinch crumbled saffron threads
2 Tbsp olive oil
3 stalks celery, cut into ½-inch pieces
2 carrots, cut into ½-inch pieces
1 small fennel bulb, trimmed and cut into ½-inch pieces (reserve feathery tops for garnish)

1 leek (white part only), thinly sliced
½ cup dry white wine
2 tomatoes, cut into ½-inch pieces
⅔ cup whipping cream
Salt and freshly ground black pepper

Rich, creamy, and full flavoured, this is one of Alain's (see page 88) favourite starters. After returning to the Lodge after a day in the cats, this soup starts the evening off nicely without spoiling your appetite for a fine dinner to come. Alain prefers mussels from PEI, which are available throughout winter. Fresh mussels should be tightly closed and ideally wrapped in netting. SERVES 6

MUSSELS Remove the mussels from the netting, scrub the shells well under cold running water, and trim off any stringy bits from shells with scissors. Discard any broken mussels or open ones that don't shut tightly when tapped sharply on the counter. In a large deep saucepan, heat oil over medium heat. Add onion and garlic. Cook for 3–5 minutes, stirring often, until onion is softened but not brown. Add mussels, wine, and bay leaves. Cover saucepan and steam for about 10 minutes or until most mussels open (discard those that don't open).

With a slotted spoon, remove mussels to a large bowl, reserving cooking liquid in saucepan. Let mussels stand until cool enough to handle. Remove mussels from shells, discarding shells. Strain cooking liquid over mussels. Refrigerate until ready to use.

SOUP In a small bowl, pour boiling water over saffron. Set aside. Strain mussels, reserving liquid. Refrigerate mussels.

In a large saucepan, heat oil over medium heat. Add celery, carrots, fennel, and leek. Cook for 5–7 minutes, stirring occasionally, until vegetables are soft but not brown. Stir in wine, reserved liquid from mussels, and saffron mixture. Bring to a boil over medium-high heat. Reduce heat to medium-low, then simmer, covered, for 10–15 minutes or until vegetables are tender. Stir in tomatoes. (Soup can be prepared ahead up to this point and refrigerated for up to 24 hours. Reheat before proceeding.)

TO SERVE Stir in cream and mussels. Reheat over medium heat, stirring occasionally, but do not boil. Taste and add salt and pepper if necessary. Ladle into shallow bowls. Garnish with reserved fennel tops.

Chickpea-Spinach Soup with Tahini

2 Tbsp olive oil
1 onion, finely diced
3 cloves garlic, minced
2 tsp ground coriander
2 tsp ground cumin
8 cups vegetable stock or water

2 medium potatoes, cut
    into chunks
2 cups cooked chickpeas
3 cups chopped fresh spinach,
    tough stems removed
3 Tbsp tahini

1 Tbsp soy sauce
¼ tsp freshly ground
    black pepper
Finely chopped parsley
    for garnish

Although popular with everyone who stays at the Lodge, this hearty soup is a particular favourite of the resort's vegan guests. Tahini is a paste made from sesame seeds and can be found in the health food sections of most large supermarkets. **SERVES 10**

In a large saucepan, heat oil over medium heat. Add onion and garlic. Cook for about 5 minutes, stirring often, until soft but not brown. Add coriander and cumin. Cook, stirring, for 2 minutes or until fragrant. Add stock and potatoes, then bring to a boil over high heat. Reduce heat to medium-low, then simmer, covered, for 20 minutes or until potatoes are almost tender.

Stir in chickpeas. Cook, covered, for about 5 minutes or until potatoes are tender. Stir in spinach, tahini, soy sauce, and pepper. Cook for 2 minutes or until spinach wilts.

Taste and add more soy sauce and pepper if necessary. Ladle into soup bowls. Garnish with parsley.

Curried Lentil and Vegetable Soup

1 cup lentils
3 Tbsp canola oil
1 large onion, finely diced
3 cloves garlic, minced
3 Tbsp curry powder
2 tsp chili powder

1 tsp salt
1 cup dry white wine
8 cups vegetable stock or water
1 stalk lemongrass
2 stalks celery, finely diced
2 carrots, finely diced

1 sweet potato, peeled
    and diced
1 can (14 oz) unsweetened
    coconut milk
Freshly ground black pepper
Fresh basil, for garnish

Tasty whether made with green or red lentils, this is a robust, filling soup for cold winter days. Substitute whatever vegetables are in season, and use hot, medium, or mild curry powder according to your taste. **SERVES 8**

Rinse lentils under cold water until water runs clear. If using green lentils, cook in a saucepan of simmering water for 1 hour or until tender. Drain well and set aside.

In a large saucepan, heat oil over medium-high heat. Add onion and garlic. Cook for about 5 minutes, stirring often, until soft but not brown. Add curry powder, chili powder, and salt. Cook, stirring, for 2 minutes or until fragrant. Stir in wine. Bring to a boil, using a wooden spoon to scrape any browned bits from bottom of saucepan. Stir in stock and lentils.

With a hammer or the handle of a sturdy knife, pound lemongrass to break up the fibres and release the flavour. Add lemongrass to saucepan. Bring to a boil over high heat. Reduce heat to medium-low, then simmer, covered, for 45 minutes or until lentils are almost tender.

Add celery, carrots, and sweet potato to saucepan. Bring back to a boil over medium-high heat. Reduce heat to medium-low, then simmer, covered, for 15–20 minutes or until vegetables and lentils are tender.

Remove and discard lemongrass. Stir in coconut milk. Reheat over medium, stirring occasionally, but do not boil. Taste and add pepper and more salt if necessary. Garnish with chopped fresh basil.

Trio of Mushrooms Soup

2 Tbsp olive oil
1 large onion, finely diced
2 stalks celery, finely diced
3 cloves garlic, minced
1 tsp paprika
1 tsp salt
1 lb button mushrooms, diced

1 lb oyster or chanterelle
   mushrooms, diced
3 portobello mushroom
   caps, diced
8 cups vegetable stock
   (see page 176) or water

3 large potatoes, peeled and
   cut into 1-inch pieces
Freshly ground black pepper
Finely chopped parsley or
   paprika for garnish

All guests, but especially those who are lactose intolerant, are amazed that a soup this rich and creamy contains no dairy products. **SERVES 8**

In a large saucepan, heat oil over medium heat. Add onion, celery, and garlic. Cook for 5 minutes, stirring often, until soft but not brown. Add paprika and salt. Cook, stirring, for 1 minute or until fragrant. Add button, oyster, and portobello mushrooms. Cook, stirring, for 5 minutes or until mushrooms release some of their liquid. Stir in stock and potatoes. Bring to a boil over high heat. Reduce heat to medium-low, then simmer, covered, for 15–20 minutes or until potatoes start to disintegrate and turn to mush.

In a blender (not a food processor) or using an immersion blender, purée soup until smooth. Return to saucepan and reheat over medium, stirring occasionally.

Taste and add pepper and more salt if necessary. Ladle into soup bowls. Garnish with parsley or ground paprika.

Chilled Green Pea Soup
with Roasted Barley Pilaf

SOUP
4 cups water
1⅓ cups granulated sugar
1 Tbsp coarse salt
4 cups shelled green peas
    or frozen peas

ROASTED BARLEY PILAF
Vegetable oil for greasing
¾ cup pearl barley
1 Tbsp butter
½ cup finely diced carrot

⅓ cup finely diced red onion
⅓ cup finely diced celery
1 clove garlic, minced
⅓ cup dry white wine
2 sprigs thyme
1 bay leaf
¼ tsp each salt and freshly
    ground black pepper
2 cups chicken or vegetable
    stock, or 1 cup each apple
    juice and water

BRANDY BUTTER & GARNISH
½ cup butter
½ cup minced shallots
1 Tbsp packed brown sugar
2 Tbsp brandy
Salt and freshly ground
    black pepper
8 oz foie gras, cut into
    8 very thin slices (see
    recipe introduction)
Whipping cream for garnish
Finely chopped chives
    for garnish

On days when it's just too warm for a hot soup, this chilled soup is the perfect start to a summer dinner. For the luxurious garnish, choose French or Quebec foie gras, wrap it tightly in cheesecloth, and chill well before slicing it as thinly as possible with a large, very sharp knife. **SERVES 4**

SOUP In a large saucepan, stir together water and sugar. Bring to a boil. Add peas and cook for 4 minutes (6 minutes for frozen). Using a strainer, remove peas from saucepan (do not discard cooking liquid). Rinse peas thoroughly under cold water.

In a blender (not a food processor), combine peas and 2 cups reserved cooking liquid. Blend until smooth, adding more cooking liquid if soup seems too thick. Rub purée through a fine sieve into a medium bowl, discarding solids from the sieve and any remaining cooking liquid. Refrigerate.

ROASTED BARLEY PILAF Lightly oil a large skillet, then heat over medium heat. Add barley. "Roast" for about 15 minutes, stirring constantly, until golden brown. Set aside.

In a large saucepan, melt butter over medium heat. Add carrot, onion, celery, and garlic. Cook, stirring, for about 4 minutes or until vegetables are starting to soften. Stir in barley. Cook, stirring, for 1 minute. Stir in wine, thyme, bay leaf, and salt and pepper,

then bring to a boil over high heat. Add stock. Bring back to a boil. Reduce heat to medium-low, then simmer, covered, for about 30 minutes or until barley is tender, adding more stock if the pilaf looks too dry. Taste and add more salt and pepper if necessary. Keep warm until ready to serve.

BRANDY BUTTER In a small skillet, melt butter over medium heat. Add shallots. Cook for 3–5 minutes, stirring often, until softened but not brown. Sprinkle with sugar. Cook, stirring, for 1 minute or until sugar melts. Add brandy. Bring to a boil, using a wooden spoon to scrape up any browned bits from bottom of skillet. Taste and add salt and pepper if necessary. Keep warm until ready to serve.

TO SERVE Spoon warm roasted barley pilaf in the centre of 4 large shallow bowls. Pour chilled soup around each portion. Fan 2 slices of foie gras over each portion of pilaf. Drizzle with a little brandy butter and whipping cream. Garnish with chives.

Yan Thereian
FORMER HEAD CHEF

"I STARTED WORKING IN A RESTAURANT AT 13. When I finished high school I started university, studying Poli Sci. After a year I quit and went to a two-year chef program."

Yan pauses, obviously thinking about the transition from academics to food. He continues, his soft voice carrying only a hint of Quebecois.

"After graduating, I started at Toqué! in Montréal under Normand Laprise. He's a rather famous chef, and that started me on my own path.

"After a bit I moved west with an itch to head my own kitchen.

"At the Lodge, no one tried to imitate anything, we were always cooking up a new adventure. Everyone shared. It was a wonderful kitchen to work in.

Laughing at the memory, he continues, "A group of people passionate about our work, the old folks, the new folks, and the experiences. When I joined the Lodge kitchen, I already had my Red Seal. The Lodge encouraged me and helped me to gain my Gold Seal."

"When you go up to the Lodge, something changes at the old growth cedar forest. The feeling. The sense there is a difference. The Lodge is special."

As we are finishing, before he gets up to leave, he holds his hand out, pausing. "There is one more thing I want to say. I am grateful and humble about my years at Island Lake Lodge. It was the most rewarding adventure I've ever had. We created something new and special every night."

Marinated Salmon with Fennel Salad

MARINATED SALMON

1 salmon fillet with skin
  (about 2 lb; preferably
  coho or sockeye)
⅔ cup black peppercorns
½ cup fennel seeds
⅓ cup coriander seeds
¾ cup salt
½ cup granulated sugar

FENNEL SALAD

Canola oil for deep-frying
30–40 drained capers
1 English cucumber, trimmed
1 medium carrot, trimmed
2 fennel bulbs, trimmed and cut
  into thin strips
1 shallot, minced
2 Tbsp olive oil

1 Tbsp each finely chopped
  parsley, fresh basil, and
  dillweed
1 Tbsp fresh lemon juice
1 tsp grainy mustard
¼ tsp each salt and freshly
  ground black pepper

In the west we are blessed with an abundance of salmon. We only use fresh wild fish at the Lodge because the flesh is firmer and contains no added chemicals. **SERVES 4–6**

MARINATED SALMON Rinse salmon under cold running water, then pat dry. Remove any visible bones with clean tweezers.

With a large mortar and pestle or in a food processor, crush peppercorns, fennel seeds, and coriander seeds until cracked. In a medium bowl, stir together peppercorn mixture, salt, and sugar.

Place salmon skin side down in a shallow dish large enough to hold it without folding. Spoon peppercorn mixture over meaty side of fillet to cover it completely. Refrigerate, covered, for 36 hours.

Scrape off peppercorn mixture. Remove salmon from dish. Rinse under cold running water to remove any excess peppercorn mixture. Pat dry with paper towels. Refrigerate, covered, until ready to serve.

FENNEL SALAD Pour canola oil into a small skillet to a depth of 1 inch. Heat oil over medium-high heat until a candy thermometer registers 250°F–265°F. Pat capers very dry on paper towels. Add capers to oil. Fry for 8–10 minutes or until capers open like small flowers. With a slotted spoon, remove capers from skillet. Drain on a plate lined with paper towel.

Using a mandoline slicer, cut cucumber and carrot into long thin ribbons, discarding cucumber's central core of seeds. Put cucumber, carrot, fennel, and shallot in a large bowl of ice water. Set aside for 20 minutes. Drain well, then pat very dry.

In a large bowl, whisk together olive oil, parsley, basil, dillweed, lemon juice, mustard, and salt and pepper. Add vegetables, then toss well. Taste and add more salt and pepper if necessary. Divide salad among 4–6 plates.

TO SERVE Using a large, flexible sharp knife and starting from the tail end of the fillet, shave very thin slices from salmon. Form a ring with the salmon using a round mould or glass and arrange salad inside (pictured). Or, arrange salmon slices on top of each portion of salad, dividing evenly. Garnish with fried capers.

Ahi Tuna Niçoise Salad

BLACK-OLIVE TAPENADE
½ cup grated Parmesan cheese
½ cup olive oil
15 large pitted kalamata olives
1 clove garlic, coarsely chopped
3 large basil leaves
¼ tsp each salt and freshly
    ground black pepper

DRESSING
¼ cup champagne vinegar
    or a good-quality white
    wine vinegar

1 egg yolk
10 drained capers, minced
1 anchovy fillet, minced
1 tsp liquid honey
¼ tsp each salt and freshly
    ground black pepper
⅓ cup hazelnut or sunflower oil

SALAD
8 tiny new potatoes, scrubbed
12 green beans, trimmed
12 quail eggs

4 fillets fresh ahi tuna loin
    (each about 3½ oz)
4 cups washed and dried
    organic baby lettuce and
    butter lettuce leaves
2 heirloom tomatoes, cut into
    wedges or cubes
Fresh cracked black
    peppercorns to taste
Fleur de sel to taste
Edible flowers for garnish

This classic tuna salad is always a guest favourite. Light yet with an interesting mix of flavours and textures, every bite is a pleasant surprise. If you can find purple-coloured "green" beans, use them instead. SERVES 4

BLACK-OLIVE TAPENADE In a mini-chopper, combine Parmesan cheese, oil, olives, garlic, basil, and salt and pepper. Process until fairly smooth. Taste and add more salt and pepper if necessary. (Tapenade can be refrigerated for up to 2 weeks.)

DRESSING In a small bowl, whisk together vinegar, egg yolk, capers, anchovy, honey, and salt and pepper until well combined. Slowly whisk in oil until slightly thickened.

SALAD Place potatoes in a medium saucepan of cold water. Bring to a boil over high heat. Add green beans. Simmer, covered, for about 5 minutes or until potatoes and beans are just tender. Drain well. Rinse under cold running water, then drain again. Cut potatoes into wedges or cubes.

Place quail eggs in a small saucepan of cold water over high heat. After 7 minutes, remove saucepan from heat. Drain well. Rinse under cold running water and drain again. Remove shells from eggs.

Just before serving, spread black-olive tapenade on both sides of each piece of tuna. Heat a large non-stick skillet over medium-high heat. Cook tuna for about 1 minute on each side. (Do not overcook. Tuna should remain coral-coloured in centre.) Remove tuna to a large plate.

TO SERVE Divide lettuce among 4 plates. Top with potatoes, green beans, quail eggs, and tomatoes, dividing evenly. Set a piece of tuna on each salad. Whisk dressing, then drizzle over each salad. Sprinkle with cracked black peppercorns and fleur de sel. Garnish with edible flowers.

Belgian Endive Salad
with Oka Cheese and Walnuts

4 Belgian endive
¼ cup fresh lemon juice
1 ripe pear
1 Tbsp mustard
1 Tbsp white wine vinegar

¼ tsp each salt and freshly
   ground black pepper
3 Tbsp canola oil
4 oz Oka cheese, coarsely
   shredded or diced

2 shallots, minced
½ cup walnut halves, toasted
2 Tbsp finely chopped parsley
Red wine syrup (see page 177)

This Canadian adaptation of a popular European classic marries very different flavours and textures in perfect balance. Fresh endive should be crisp, unblemished, and pale in colour. **SERVES 4**

Wash and dry endive. Cut each in half lengthwise, then cut out cores. Cut each endive crosswise into 1-inch slices. In a medium bowl, toss endive with 2 Tbsp lemon juice.

Slice pear thinly lengthwise, cutting out core. In a small bowl, toss pear with remaining lemon juice.

In a large bowl, whisk together mustard, vinegar, and salt and pepper. Slowly whisk in oil until slightly thickened.

Just before serving, whisk dressing. Drain endive. Add endive to dressing, along with cheese and shallots. Toss gently. Taste and add more salt and pepper if necessary. Divide salad among 4 plates. Sprinkle each serving with walnuts and parsley. Garnish with drained pear slices and a drizzle of red wine syrup.

Salad Barigoule

SALAD

2 cups washed and dried
    spinach leaves, tough
    stems removed
2 cups shelled soy beans or
    flageolets, blanched
2 large heirloom tomatoes,
    diced
1 sweet onion, thinly sliced
3 cooked artichoke hearts, diced
3 medium carrots, thinly sliced

3 cooked hearts of palm, sliced
2 stalks celery, finely diced
4 radishes, sliced
1 clove garlic, minced

DRESSING

1 lemon
½ cup olive oil
¼ cup champagne vinegar
    or good-quality white
    wine vinegar

4 large basil leaves,
    finely chopped
1 tsp granulated sugar
1 tsp finely chopped
    fresh thyme
¼ tsp each salt and freshly
    ground black pepper
Washed and dried butter
    lettuce leaves, or steamed
    basmati rice

In the warmer months, the organic garden of Cincott Farms (see page 57) provides the Lodge with a medley of fresh vegetables for this versatile summer salad. Serve over greens or even steamed rice.
SERVES 4–6

SALAD In a large bowl, toss together spinach, soy beans, tomatoes, onion, artichoke hearts, carrots, hearts of palm, celery, radishes, and garlic until well combined.

DRESSING Squeeze juice from lemon. In a small bowl, whisk together lemon juice, olive oil, vinegar, basil, sugar, thyme, and salt and pepper until smooth.

TO SERVE Add dressing to vegetables. Toss well. Taste and add more salt and pepper if necessary. Serve over fresh crisp butter lettuce or steamed basmati rice.

Smoked Duck Salad

SMOKED DUCK
4 whole duck breasts
1 lemon
2 cups Japanese soy sauce
2 cups apple cider
   or apple juice
3 bay leaves
Apple or alder wood chips
1 Tbsp canola oil
Cinnamon to taste

Salt and freshly ground
   black pepper

BROTH
4 cups chicken stock
   (see page 176)
¾ cup sliced fresh ginger
1 bunch green onions,
   thinly sliced
3 stalks lemongrass, chopped

SALAD
1 cup slivered snow peas
1 cup slivered carrots
1 cup slivered parsnips
1 Tbsp rice wine vinegar
¼ tsp each salt and freshly
   ground black pepper
Soy sauce, sesame oil,
   and fresh lemon juice
   for drizzling

Enjoy this light duck salad in the summer on the deck with a glass of Pinot Noir. **SERVES 4**

SMOKED DUCK Trim off any excess fat from edges of duck breasts. With a sharp knife, score skin and fat of each breast in a cross-hatch pattern.

Squeeze juice from lemon. In a large non-reactive bowl, stir together lemon juice, soy sauce, apple cider, and bay leaves. Add duck breasts. Refrigerate, covered, for at least 8 hours or overnight.

Remove breasts from marinade, discarding marinade. Arrange duck breasts on a wire rack set over a rimmed baking sheet. Refrigerate, uncovered, for 30–40 minutes.

Smoke duck breasts in a smoker or on a barbecue, with apple or alder wood chips, for 3 hours or until flavour is infused but the breasts remain uncooked, or follow manufacturer's instructions.

Preheat the oven to 400°F. Heat a large heavy ovenproof skillet over medium-high heat, then add oil. Season duck breasts liberally with cinnamon and a little salt and pepper. Place duck breasts fat side down in skillet. Cook for 30 seconds. Reduce heat to low. Cook for 3–5 minutes or until breasts have rendered some of their fat, basting breasts with the juices in the skillet. Pour excess fat from skillet. Transfer skillet to oven. Cook for 5–7 minutes or until a meat thermom-

eter inserted into thickest breast registers 120°F for rare. Remove breasts to a cutting board. Tent loosely with foil and let rest for 5 minutes.

BROTH Meanwhile, in a large saucepan, stir together chicken stock, ginger, green onions, and lemongrass. Bring to a boil over high heat. Reduce heat to medium-high, then boil for about 10 minutes or until stock reduces to 2 cups. Pour through a fine strainer. Return stock to saucepan. Keep warm until ready to serve.

SALAD In a medium saucepan of boiling, salted water, cook snow peas, carrots, and parsnips for 1 minute. Drain well. Rinse under cold running water and drain again. Pat dry. Just before serving, toss vegetables in a medium bowl with vinegar and salt and pepper. Spoon salad onto each of 4 plates.

TO SERVE Slice each duck breast diagonally into 5 slices. Fan 1 breast alongside each portion of salad. Pool a little broth onto each plate under breast. Drizzle each portion of duck and salad with a little soy sauce, sesame oil, and lemon juice.

Appetizers

Phyllo-Wrapped Oka with Blueberry Salsa

BLUEBERRY SALSA
½ cup fresh, or frozen and
    thawed, blueberries
2 plum tomatoes, peeled,
    seeded, and diced
1 red onion, finely diced
¼ cup olive oil
2 cloves garlic, minced

1 small jalapeño, seeded
    and minced
2 Tbsp fresh lime juice
1 Tbsp finely chopped cilantro
1 Tbsp shredded fresh basil
Pinch ground cumin
Salt and freshly ground
    black pepper

PHYLLO-WRAPPED OKA
4 oz Oka cheese
2 sheets frozen phyllo
    pastry, thawed
2 Tbsp olive oil
4 pinches cornmeal
1 tsp finely chopped parsley
1 tsp finely chopped
    fresh oregano

This comforting appetizer is served often during winters at the Lodge, with the cheese filling and the fruit salsa varying according to what's available. **SERVES 4**

BLUEBERRY SALSA In a small saucepan, heat blueberries over medium heat just until they release some of their juices. Tip blueberries and juices into a medium bowl. Stir in tomatoes, onion, olive oil, garlic, jalapeño, lime juice, cilantro, basil, and cumin. Let stand at room temperature for 45 minutes to allow flavours to blend. Taste and add salt and pepper if necessary.

PHYLLO-WRAPPED OKA Preheat the oven to 375°F. Cut cheese into 4 even-sized rectangles. Lay 1 sheet of phyllo on work surface. Brush phyllo lightly with 1 Tbsp olive oil. Sprinkle with a pinch of cornmeal. Top with second sheet of phyllo. Cut phyllo into 4 even strips.

Put 1 piece of cheese at end of each strip. Sprinkle each piece of cheese evenly with parsley and oregano. Roll up pastry to enclose each piece of cheese, tucking in the ends of the pastry to seal.

Place phyllo packages on a greased baking sheet and brush with remaining olive oil. Bake for 10–15 minutes or until pastry is golden and cheese barely starts to ooze.

TO SERVE Put 1 phyllo package on each of 4 plates. Let stand for 2 minutes. Serve with the salsa on the side. Or place one-quarter of the salsa in a 3-inch round cookie cutter on each plate. Remove the cookie cutter and top with the phyllo packages.

Mark Butcher
SOUS CHEF

STANDING NEXT TO THE CHOPPING BLOCK, wearing his cap, Mark Butcher looks more like a Cockney cabbie from the '70s than a sous chef in the mountains of B.C. Between the staccato beat of his knife he explains how he ended up at Island Lake Lodge.

"I started cooking with my Nana. She was always cooking." He laughs. "There's a picture of me at four or five making meatballs with her. She's standing back, with her hand up, and I'm about to fire one at her." He stops chopping and cocks his arm back.

"I always worked in restaurants, bars. Started at 15. Now it's been 15 years."

He pauses again from the chopping. "I left Fernie and went to the George Brown College 12-month program. Came back, met Farkas and started working at Island Lake Lodge. It's the only place in the Valley I wanted to work and I was lucky.

He looks over to me.

"When I started, cooking didn't have the kind of 'cool' it holds now. Today people consider it a 'cool' profession. Look at all the TV shows and books."

He shakes his head, clearly wondering.

"It's all I ever wanted to do."

He turns back to his board and the staccato beat begins anew.

MARK'S RECIPES

- Trilogy of Quail Eggs Benedict (page 13)
- Potato-Crusted Halibut with Champagne Mayonnaise (page 85)
- Island Lake Lodge Fresh Fettuccine (page 96)
- Poached Rack of Lamb with Mint Gastrique (page 132)
- Funnel Cakes with Ice Cream and Berry Compote (page 154)

Shallot Tarte Tatin with Brie Mousse

BRIE MOUSSE
¾ cup cubed brie cheese with rind
⅔ cup whipping cream
¼ cup water
1½ tsp unflavoured powdered gelatin
1 Tbsp finely chopped chives
Salt and freshly ground black pepper

TARTE TATIN
2 cups milk
4 medium shallots, peeled
3 sprigs thyme
1 tsp freshly ground black pepper
Salt to taste
¾ cup (approx.) red wine
Half 397-gram package frozen puff pastry, thawed

2 Tbsp clarified butter (see page 177)
Red wine syrup (see page 177)
1 cup mesclun mix
1 Tbsp olive oil
1 tsp balsamic vinegar

This deceptively easy appetizer features a stunning combo of red wine–braised shallots and creamy brie mousse. **SERVES 4**

BRIE MOUSSE In a heatproof bowl set over a saucepan of simmering water, stir together brie and ⅓ cup cream until brie melts and mixture is smooth. Meanwhile, in a small bowl, sprinkle gelatin over water. Let stand for 5 minutes until puffy. Set bowl in a small saucepan of simmering water. Stir until gelatin is completely dissolved.

Strain the cheese mixture into a medium bowl. Whisk in gelatin mixture until completely dissolved. Chill cheese mixture for about 3 hours or until just starting to set.

Whip remaining cream in a medium bowl until it almost holds stiff peaks. Fold whipped cream into cheese mixture until well combined. Fold in chives, and salt and pepper to taste. Refrigerate, covered, for about 3 hours or until set.

TARTE TATIN In a small saucepan, combine milk, shallots, thyme, pepper, and salt to taste. Bring to a boil over medium-high heat. Reduce heat to medium-low, then simmer, uncovered, for 20–25 minutes or until the shallots are tender. Strain, discarding thyme. Set shallots aside to cool. (Milk may be reserved for making sauces for other recipes.)

Put shallots in a small shallow non-reactive saucepan. Add enough wine to come halfway up shallots. Bring to a boil over medium-high heat. Reduce heat to medium-low, then simmer, uncovered and without disturbing shallots, until wine has almost all evaporated.

Preheat the oven to 400°F. Line a large rimmed baking sheet with parchment paper. On a lightly floured surface, roll out puff pastry to an 8-inch square. Cut pastry into four 4-inch squares. Arrange shallots, browned sides down and well apart, on baking sheet. Top each shallot with a square of pastry, centering pastry over shallot. Mould each piece of pastry over shallot. Brush pastry with clarified butter. Bake for 10–15 minutes or until pastry is puffed and golden brown.

TO SERVE Arrange 1 tarte Tatin, shallot side up, on each of 4 plates. Spoon some of the mousse alongside each tarte Tatin. Drizzle plates with red wine syrup. Toss mesclun mix with olive oil and balsamic vinegar, and pile alongside each tarte Tatin.

Baked Italian Purses

4 oz soft goat cheese,
    at room temperature
4 oz cream cheese,
    at room temperature
1 Tbsp minced sun-dried
    tomatoes

1 tsp finely chopped parsley
1 tsp finely chopped fresh basil
Salt and freshly ground
    black pepper
2 sheets frozen phyllo
    pastry, thawed

3 Tbsp olive oil
1 cup mesclun mix
1 tsp balsamic vinegar
Balsamic syrup
    (see page 177)

Goat cheese and sun-dried tomatoes baked with fresh herbs in a phyllo purse is one of the most popular tapas items on the Lodge's summer menu. If using dry-packed sun-dried tomatoes (as opposed to those packed in oil), soak them in hot water until pliable before mincing. **SERVES 4**

Preheat the oven to 375°F. Using an electric mixer (preferably a stand mixer), beat cheeses until smooth. Add tomatoes, parsley, basil, and salt and pepper to taste. Continue beating until very smooth.

Lay 1 sheet of phyllo on work surface. Brush phyllo lightly with 1 Tbsp olive oil. Top with second sheet of phyllo. Cut phyllo into 4 squares. Spoon one-quarter of cheese mixture in centre of each square. Gather up sides of each square of phyllo to enclose cheese, crimping pastry together over cheese to form little purses. Put purses on a greased baking sheet. Brush with 1 Tbsp olive oil. Bake for 10–15 minutes or until golden brown.

Put 1 phyllo purse on each of 4 plates. Toss mesclun mix with remaining olive oil and the balsamic vinegar. Pile mesclun mix alongside each purse. Drizzle each plate with balsamic syrup.

Sesame-Crusted Fish Cakes with Hot Pepper Coulis

BANANA SALSA

2 limes

5 bananas

1 each red and orange sweet
pepper, seeded and finely
diced

1 English cucumber, seeded
and finely diced

¼ cup finely diced red onion

1 Tbsp finely chopped chives

3 Tbsp sesame oil

4 sprigs cilantro

Salt and freshly ground
black pepper

HOT PEPPER COULIS

3 cups dry white wine

2 cups seeded and finely diced
banana peppers

2 roasted red peppers (see
page 177), peeled, seeded,
and stems removed

½ cup liquid honey

2 Tbsp rice vinegar

FISH CAKES

10 kaffir lime leaves

4 stalks lemongrass

1¼ lb haddock, tilapia, or
catfish fillets, finely chopped

3 Tbsp finely grated fresh
ginger

3 Tbsp sambal oelek
(Indonesian hot pepper
sauce)

1 Tbsp grated orange zest

Salt and freshly ground
black pepper

Sesame seeds for coating

2 Tbsp canola oil

On his travels, Kelly (see page 73) collects flavours to bring home and combine in unusual ways. He picked up the idea for these Asian-style fish cakes, served with a hot pepper coulis and a banana salsa, while exploring the cuisine and culture of Bali. **SERVES 4**

BANANA SALSA Squeeze juice from limes into a non-reactive bowl. Peel then chop bananas, immediately adding pieces to lime juice. Toss to coat. Stir in sweet peppers, cucumber, red onion, chives, sesame oil, cilantro, and salt and pepper to taste.

HOT PEPPER COULIS In a large saucepan, combine wine, banana peppers, roasted peppers, honey, and vinegar. Bring to a boil over medium-high heat. Reduce heat to medium, then simmer, uncovered, until most of the liquid evaporates and banana peppers are soft. Remove from the heat. Let cool slightly. Pour mixture into a food processor. Process until smooth. Strain through a fine sieve lined with cheesecloth. Set aside.

FISH CAKES Remove stems from lime leaves. Chop leaves finely. Trim 1 inch from bottom and 3 inches from top of lemongrass stalks.

Remove and discard outer husks to reveal soft inner shoot. Chop shoot finely. In a large bowl and wearing plastic gloves, gently mix together fish, lime leaves, lemongrass, ginger, sambal oelek, orange zest, and salt and pepper to taste. Form mixture into four 3-inch patties each about ¾ inch thick. Coat fish cakes all over with sesame seeds. Refrigerate until ready to cook.

Preheat the oven to 350°F. In a large ovenproof skillet, heat oil over medium-high heat. Fry fish cakes for 2–3 minutes, turning once, until sesame seeds are toasted. Transfer skillet to the oven. Cook for 10–15 minutes or until an instant-read or meat thermometer inserted into cakes registers 140°F.

TO SERVE Divide fish cakes among 4 plates. Pile banana salsa alongside each cake. Pour hot pepper coulis into 4 shooter glasses to serve with fish cakes.

Shrimp and Chickpea Fritters
with Red Pepper Mayonnaise

RED PEPPER MAYONNAISE
2 small roasted red peppers
   (see page 177)
1 egg yolk
1 tsp Dijon mustard
1 tsp red wine vinegar
1⅓ cups canola oil
Salt and freshly ground
   black pepper

SHRIMP AND CHICKPEA
FRITTERS
3 cloves garlic, unpeeled
1 lb large shrimp, peeled
   and deveined
1 can (14 oz) chickpeas,
   drained and rinsed
½ cup chickpea flour
1 egg

3 Tbsp finely chopped parsley
Salt and freshly ground
   black pepper
1½ cups canola oil

1 cup mesclun mix
1 Tbsp olive oil
1 tsp red wine vinegar

This is another popular item on the Lodge's summer tapas menu, featuring bite-sized portions of flavourful food all designed to be shared with friends. Look for chickpea flour in health food or South Asian grocery stores. SERVES 4

RED PEPPER MAYONNAISE In a mini-chopper or food processor, process roasted peppers until smooth. Rub purée through a sieve. In a medium bowl, whisk together egg yolk, mustard, and vinegar. Gradually whisk in oil in a thin stream, continuing to whisk until smooth and creamy. Whisk in roasted pepper purée, and salt and pepper to taste.

SHRIMP AND CHICKPEA FRITTERS In a small skillet over medium heat, toast garlic cloves for 5–7 minutes or until skins blacken and garlic is softened. Remove from the skillet. Let cool slightly. Pop garlic out of skins, then mince finely.

In a food processor, process shrimp and chickpeas until almost smooth. In a medium bowl, stir together shrimp mixture, garlic,

flour, egg, parsley, and salt and pepper to taste until well combined. Refrigerate, covered, until ready to cook.

Just before serving, heat oil in a large heavy skillet over high heat until a candy thermometer registers 375°F. Use 2 dessert spoons to form shrimp mixture into 18–20 oval fritters. Fry fritters a few at a time in hot oil for 3–5 minutes, turning once, until golden brown. Drain fritters on a plate lined with paper towel. Keep warm as you fry the remainder.

TO SERVE Divide fritters among 4 plates. Toss mesclun mix with olive oil and red wine vinegar. Pile mesclun mix alongside each portion of fritters. Serve with red pepper mayonnaise.

Marinated Eggplant with Shrimp Mousseline

MARINATED EGGPLANT
2 small eggplant
1 stalk lemongrass
⅓ cup sesame oil
1 Tbsp minced fresh ginger
1 Tbsp minced garlic
1 Tbsp sambal oelek (Indonesian hot pepper sauce)
½ cup rice vinegar
⅓ cup soy sauce
⅓ cup unsweetened apple juice
Granulated sugar to taste

CORN RELISH
3 ears corn, shucked

½ cup rice vinegar
1 tsp liquid honey
⅓ cup finely diced sweet
    red pepper
⅓ cup thinly sliced green onions
⅓ cup shredded fresh basil

YELLOW CURRY SAUCE
1 stalk lemongrass
3 Tbsp sesame oil
2–3 Tbsp yellow curry paste,
    to taste
1 small onion, finely diced
1 Tbsp minced garlic
1 Tbsp minced fresh ginger

1 cup unsweetened coconut milk
1 Tbsp turmeric
1 plum tomato, seeded and
    finely diced
Salt and freshly ground
    black pepper

SHRIMP MOUSSELINE
1 lb tiger shrimp, peeled
    and deveined
1 tsp salt
Cayenne pepper
Freshly ground white pepper
2 egg whites
2 cups chilled whipping cream

A fusion of east-west flavours, spicy eggplant cups hold a creamy shrimp mousse to serve with a zippy curry sauce. **SERVES 4**

MARINATED EGGPLANT Cut eggplant in half lengthwise. Hollow out centres of eggplant, leaving a ¾-inch border, forming 4 elongated "cups." Put eggplant cups, skin side down, in a shallow dish large enough to hold them in a single layer.

Trim 1 inch from bottom and 3 inches from top of lemongrass stalk. Remove and discard outer husks to reveal soft inner shoot. Chop shoot finely. In a small skillet, heat sesame oil over medium-high heat. Add lemongrass, ginger, garlic, and sambal oelek. Cook, stirring, for 2–3 minutes or until fragrant. Remove skillet from the heat. Stir in vinegar, soy sauce, apple juice, and sugar. Let cool. Drizzle vinegar mixture evenly over eggplant. Let stand at room temperature for 12 hours.

CORN RELISH In a large saucepan of boiling water, cook ears of corn for 10 minutes or until tender. Remove corn from saucepan. Cool in a bowl of ice water.

Cut kernels from ears of corn and place in a medium bowl. In a small saucepan over medium-high heat, bring vinegar and honey to a boil, then pour over corn. Stir in red pepper and green onions. Let stand at room temperature for 12 hours. Just before serving, stir in basil.

continued on next page . . .

Marinated Eggplant with Shrimp Mousseline *(continued)*

YELLOW CURRY SAUCE Trim 1 inch from bottom and 3 inches from top of lemongrass stalk. Remove and discard outer husks to reveal soft inner shoot. Chop shoot finely. In a small saucepan, heat sesame oil over medium-high heat. Add lemongrass, curry paste, onion, garlic, and ginger. Cook, stirring, for 3–5 minutes or until browned and fragrant. Stir in coconut milk and turmeric. Bring to a boil. Remove saucepan from the heat. Stir in tomato, and salt and pepper to taste. Rub through a fine sieve. Reheat before serving.

SHRIMP MOUSSELINE Reserving 4 shrimp for garnish, process the remainder in a food processor until smooth. Rub shrimp purée through a fine sieve. Return purée to food processor. Add salt, and cayenne and white pepper to taste. Process briefly. Add egg whites 1 at a time, processing after each addition until well combined. With processor running, add 1 cup cream in a thin stream. Still with processor running, gradually add remaining cream just until mixture looks silky (you may not need all the cream).

In a small skillet over medium heat, cook 1 Tbsp shrimp mousseline for 2–3 minutes, turning once, until cooked through. Taste cooked portion and add more salt, cayenne pepper, or white pepper to raw mixture as necessary.

Preheat the oven to 350°F. Remove eggplant cups from marinade, shaking off excess. Put eggplant cups in a shallow ovenproof dish large enough to hold them in a single layer. Set dish in a large shallow roasting pan. Spoon shrimp mousseline into eggplant cups, dividing evenly. Pour boiling water into roasting pan to reach halfway up sides of dish. Bake for 30–40 minutes or until eggplant cups are tender.

TO SERVE Place 1 reserved shrimp on top of each mousseline-filled eggplant cup. Return to the oven for a further 10 minutes or until shrimp are just pink and firm, and shrimp mousseline is set. Put 1 eggplant cup on each of 4 plates. Serve with corn relish and yellow curry sauce.

Organic to the Core: Cincott Farms

THE LITTLE TOWN OF HOSMER, EIGHT KILOMETRES EAST of Fernie, was once a thriving mining town. Today it is little more than a wide spot on the road with a battered hotel and a few homes. And there's also Cincott Farms, a bustling organic nursery and produce supplier, which is a vital part of the food supply at Island Lake Lodge.

Early this spring, I drove out to pick up plants to start a small kitchen herb garden in my backyard. As I drive up, Cindy greets me with a wave and a call, "I'll catch up with you in a minute!" Her arms are loaded with flats of plants.

I amble off to explore. When Cindy catches up with me, I already have a couple pots of basil and rosemary. She pulls the leaf off a nearby plant. "This is Thai basil." And then she crushes it under my nose.

"Ah, I'll take one of those."

"Oh, and try this lettuce!" She pulls off a leaf and feeds it to me. Crisp. A little spicy with a hint of anise. I take one of those too. With three fingers on each hand gripping little square pots, I wonder how much more I can handle. Without asking Cindy finds me a flat.

As I'm going through the checkout, she puts some of their jalapeño chutney on a cracker. *Oh, I'll have one of those*—and I grab a dozen organic free-range eggs. Half an hour later, I am loading the car, my garden basically all set up.

Over the last eight years, Cindy and Scott forged a vital link with the community and with Island Lake Lodge. Every spring, the Lodge chefs meet with Cindy and Scott to discuss what worked the year before and to taste any new offerings. Cindy sets up a plot dedicated to the Lodge program. And once or twice a week, they deliver the week's pick of the farm to the Lodge.

The variety of organic produce and the level to which they are attuned to customer service draws people back time after time. And, of course, the chutney's to die for.

Pan-Seared Digby Scallops

SWEET PICKLED ONION AND FENNEL
2 fennel bulbs, trimmed
1 medium red onion, peeled
½ cup granulated sugar
½ cup red wine vinegar
3 Tbsp pickling spice
Salt and freshly ground
   black pepper

SPICY ROUILLE
1 clove garlic, unpeeled
1 lemon
2 egg yolks
½ cup extra virgin canola oil
2 Tbsp sambal oelek (Indonesian
   hot pepper sauce)
Salt and freshly ground
   black pepper

PAN-SEARED SCALLOPS
12 Digby or other fresh large
   scallops
1 Tbsp canola oil
Salt and freshly ground
   white pepper

A spicy garlic rouille, *similar to mayo, and sweet homemade pickles turn simple seared scallops into a special treat.* **SERVES 4**

SWEET PICKLED ONION AND FENNEL Cut fennel and onion into wafer-thin slices, using a mandoline slicer. Place fennel and onion in a large non-reactive bowl.

In a small saucepan, stir together sugar, vinegar, and pickling spice. Bring to a boil over high heat. Reduce heat to very low, then let steep for 1 hour. Strain vinegar mixture, discarding spice. Return vinegar mixture to saucepan. Bring to a boil over high heat, then pour over fennel and onion. Let stand at room temperature for 1 hour. Season with salt and pepper to taste.

SPICY ROUILLE In a small skillet over medium heat, toast garlic clove for 5–7 minutes or until skin blackens and garlic is softened. Remove from the skillet. Let cool slightly. Pop garlic out of skin, then mince finely. Squeeze juice from lemon. In a medium bowl and using an electric mixer, beat lemon juice, garlic, and egg yolks for about 5 minutes or until light and fluffy. Continuing to beat, add oil in a thin stream. Beat in sambal oelek. Season with salt and pepper to taste. Refrigerate until ready to serve.

PAN-SEARED SCALLOPS Remove the tough tendon on side of each scallop. Wash scallops well in cold water. Pat dry. In a large heavy skillet, heat oil over high heat. Sprinkle scallops with salt and pepper. Sear for about 1 minute on each side or until golden brown (do not overcook).

TO SERVE Divide scallops among 4 plates. Garnish with the spicy rouille and sweet pickled onion and fennel.

Wild Sockeye Salmon Tartare
with Spicy Guacamole and Taro Chips

SPICY GUACAMOLE
2 lemons
3 ripe Haas avocados
1 sweet red pepper, seeded
   and finely diced
1 jalapeño, seeded and minced
2 Tbsp finely chopped cilantro
Salt and freshly ground
   black pepper

TARO CHIPS
1 medium taro root
Canola oil for deep-frying

SALMON TARTARE
¼ cup fresh lemon juice
1 egg yolk
2 Tbsp drained, minced capers
2 Tbsp minced red onion
   or shallot

2 Tbsp finely chopped
   fresh dillweed
1 Tbsp smooth Dijon mustard
1 Tbsp liquid honey
¾ lb wild boneless, skinless
   sockeye salmon fillet
Salt and freshly ground
   black pepper
Finely chopped cilantro
   for garnish

The West Coast heads south in this pairing of wild salmon and spicy guacamole. When preparing the salmon tartare, *cut the fillet into the smallest pieces possible without turning the fish to mush, and let stand in its marinade for no longer than 10 minutes before serving, or the acid in the lemon juice will "cook" the fish. Taro root is a starchy vegetable popular in the Caribbean. If you can't find it, substitute regular or sweet potato.* **SERVES 4**

SPICY GUACAMOLE Squeeze juice from lemons into a medium bowl. Peel, pit, then finely chop avocados, immediately adding pieces to lemon juice. Toss to coat. Add red pepper, jalapeño, cilantro, and salt and pepper to taste. Stir gently. Let stand at room temperature for at least 30 minutes for flavours to blend (a couple of hours will make it taste even richer).

TARO CHIPS Peel taro root. Slice as thinly as possible (use a mandoline slicer if you have one). Pour oil into a large deep saucepan to a depth of 2 inches. Heat over high heat until a candy thermometer registers 350°F. Pat taro slices dry on paper towels, then fry in small batches for 1–2 minutes or until golden and crisp. Drain on a plate lined with paper towel.

SALMON TARTARE In a small bowl, stir together lemon juice, egg yolk, capers, red onion, dillweed, mustard, and honey until well combined. Set aside. With a sharp knife, cut salmon into ¼-inch strips, then dice strips crosswise. Add salmon to lemon juice mixture. Stir gently. Season with salt and pepper to taste. Refrigerate for 5–10 minutes before serving (no longer or lemon juice will "cook" the fish).

TO SERVE Spoon a little guacamole on each of 4 plates, then top with a layer of taro chips. Spoon a little salmon tartare on top of chips, then repeat this layering twice to create a tower. Repeat with remaining ingredients. Garnish with cilantro.

Roasted Garlic Foie Gras Torchon with Crostini and Pear Gastrique

FOIE GRAS TORCHON
1 whole foie gras
1 tsp pink salt
1 tsp granulated sugar
20 cloves garlic, peeled
¼ cup butter, melted
12 cups chicken stock
    (see page 176)

PEAR GASTRIQUE
½ cup packed brown sugar
½ cup pear vinegar
2 ripe pears, peeled, cored, and
    thinly sliced crosswise

CROSTINI
2 small ciabatta buns
5 sprigs rosemary
⅓ cup olive oil
Salt and freshly ground
    black pepper

Torchon is French for "towel," and refers to the method of cooking foie gras in cheesecloth to form a neat sausage shape. Gastrique is a syrupy reduction of sugar, vinegar, and often fruit—in this case, pears—which forms a sweet and tart foil for the richness of the foie gras. If you can't find pear vinegar, substitute good-quality apple cider vinegar. SERVES 6–8

FOIE GRAS TORCHON Let foie gras stand at room temperature for 1 hour (this makes it easier to work with). Separate the 2 lobes where they break naturally. Remove any visible veins. Set aside the few small pieces of foie gras that break off. Spread out foie gras and sprinkle with salt and sugar. Wrap tightly in plastic wrap. Refrigerate overnight. Refrigerate small pieces separately.

Preheat the oven to 350°F. In a small bowl, toss garlic cloves with butter until well coated. Wrap loosely in foil. Roast for about 1 hour or until very soft. Let garlic cool to room temperature. In a mini-chopper, process garlic with reserved small pieces of foie gras until smooth.

Unwrap foie gras, then spread it out on a large sheet of parchment paper. Spoon garlic purée down the centre to form a stuffing. Using the parchment paper to roll foie gras, form it into a cylinder, about 6 inches long and 3 inches in diameter. Discard parchment.

Wrap foie gras very tightly in a double layer of cheesecloth. Tie butcher's twine very tightly around foie gras, binding it like a roast.

Have ready a large bowl of ice water. In a large shallow saucepan, bring the stock to a boil over medium-high heat. Add cheesecloth-wrapped foie gras. Poach in the boiling stock for 90–120 seconds. Remove foie gras and immediately place in ice water to cool. When cool enough to handle, re-tie string to tighten it. Hang foie gras in fridge overnight

PEAR GASTRIQUE In a small saucepan, stir together sugar and vinegar. Bring to a boil over medium-high heat. Add pears. Reduce heat to medium-low, then simmer, uncovered, for 30 minutes or until pears are tender. With a slotted spoon, remove pears to a bowl. Set aside. Continue to simmer sugar mixture until reduced and syrupy. Pour over pears. Let cool completely.

CROSTINI Preheat the oven to 375°F. Cut ciabatta buns into thin diagonal slices. Strip leaves from rosemary sprigs. With a mortar and pestle, pound rosemary leaves to a paste. Add olive oil, and salt and pepper to taste. Continue pounding the mixture until well combined. Lay ciabatta slices on a large baking sheet. Brush with rosemary oil. Bake for about 5 minutes or until golden but not completely dried out.

TO SERVE Unwrap foie gras torchon. Cut crosswise into 1-inch slices. The outside of the foie gras will have oxidized and turned grey. To remove the oxidized layer, trim rounds with a cookie cutter slightly smaller than the slices of foie gras. Using a slightly larger cookie cutter, cut rounds from pear slices. Top each crostini with a pear slice and a slice of foie gras. Finish with a drizzle of pear gastrique.

Keith Farkas
FORMER HEAD CHEF

IN HIS EARLY 30S, KEITH IS A SLIGHT MAN with quick motions. Watching him move around the kitchen, you want to say, "Stop. Do that again. Slower." You want to watch, to dissect his movements.

"I started out working in a crappy family restaurant as a dishwasher. After a bit I moved up to prep cook. Two and half years of that and I moved to Banff to ski." He laughs as he thinks back. "There I started working with real chefs and that was an eye opener.

"I thought to myself, *Hey, I can do this.* I'd been accepted to engineering school back east and passed. I didn't want to leave. I wanted to cook. So I stayed."

When Keith decided to enter the Red Seal Certificate program, he still didn't want to leave Banff to go to school. With over 12,000 documented hours, he picked up the books, studied hard, challenged the test, and passed.

"The whole organic, local concept totally makes sense at the Lodge, and in general."

He talks of the head chefs he worked with at the Lodge. "Alain, he was more classic. Yan, wild. Kelly has great presentation and vision.

"In general, I'd call the cuisine 'freestyle.'"

Bocconcini and Eggplant "Ravioli" with Braised Mushrooms

RAVIOLI

1 large eggplant

2 Tbsp coarse salt

1 whole roasted head garlic (see page 177)

⅓ cup olive oil

2 medium shallots, minced

1 Tbsp finely chopped parsley

1 tsp finely chopped fresh thyme

1 tsp finely chopped fresh oregano

¼ cup all-purpose flour

12 small balls bocconcini

Salt and freshly ground black pepper

BRAISED MUSHROOMS

1 Tbsp butter

4 medium cipollini onions, peeled and quartered

3 oz cremini mushrooms, quartered

3 oz oyster mushrooms, cut into matchstick strips

1 large portobello mushroom cap, diced

½ cup dry sherry

3 Tbsp chicken stock (see page 176)

3 sprigs thyme

Salt and freshly ground black pepper

2 plum tomatoes, peeled, seeded, and diced

¼ cup truffle oil

1 tsp finely chopped chives

Reduced balsamic vinegar for garnish

This starter also makes a wonderful vegetarian dinner for two to four people. For a heartier main course, serve with Parmesan-cheese polenta. **SERVES 6**

RAVIOLI Cut eggplant lengthwise into 12 very thin slices, discarding trimmings. Put eggplant in a large colander and sprinkle with coarse salt. Let stand for 30 minutes.

Pop garlic from skins into a small bowl, then mash until smooth. In a small saucepan, heat 1 Tbsp oil over medium-high heat. Add shallots. Cook, stirring, for 3–5 minutes or until soft but not brown. Stir in garlic, parsley, thyme, and oregano. Remove from the heat and set aside.

Rinse eggplant slices and pat very dry. In a large bowl, toss eggplant with flour until slices are well coated. Heat ¼ cup oil in a large skillet over medium-high heat. Fry eggplant slices in small batches for 3–5 minutes or until golden. As each batch is ready, lay slices out in a single layer on a lightly floured surface.

Drain cheese and pat dry. Place 1 tsp shallot mixture and 1 cheese ball at one end of each eggplant slice. Sprinkle with salt and pepper to taste. Roll up each eggplant slice, folding in sides to enclose cheese and make a tight package. Refrigerate until ready to cook.

BRAISED MUSHROOMS In a large skillet, melt butter over medium heat. Add onions. Cook, stirring, for 7–9 minutes or until onions are soft but not brown. Add cremini, oyster, and portobello mushrooms. Stir to coat mushrooms in the onion mixture. Add sherry, stock, and thyme. Bring to a boil over medium-high heat. Reduce heat to low, then simmer, covered, for 20 minutes or until mushrooms are tender. Season with salt and pepper to taste. Stir in tomatoes, truffle oil, and chives. Keep warm until ready to serve.

Preheat the oven to 375°F. Put ravioli on a rimmed baking sheet lined with parchment paper. Brush with remaining olive oil. Bake, uncovered, for 10–12 minutes or until heated through.

TO SERVE Divide among 6 plates. Spoon the braised mushrooms alongside. Drizzle with reduced balsamic vinegar.

Ménage à Trois

PEPPERED TROUT GRAVLAX

6 Tbsp coarse salt

3 Tbsp cracked black peppercorns

3 Tbsp granulated sugar

8 oz boneless rainbow trout fillets, with skin

1 lemon, thinly sliced

2 sprigs tarragon

PICKLED FENNEL

1 large fennel bulb, trimmed and cut into matchstick strips

1 cup dry white wine

⅔ cup white wine vinegar

½ cup granulated sugar

1 Tbsp coarse salt

2 cloves garlic, peeled

2 tsp freshly ground black pepper

1 bay leaf

LEMON CHUTNEY

1 small onion, finely diced

¼ cup fresh lemon juice

2 Tbsp white wine vinegar

2 cloves garlic, thinly sliced

1 leek (white part only), finely diced

3 Tbsp granulated sugar

1 Tbsp cornstarch

1 Tbsp cold water

4 large basil leaves, shredded

Salt and freshly ground black pepper

4 lemons, peeled and segmented

SAUTÉED SHRIMP

⅓ cup butter

3 shallots, minced

8 extra-large shrimp, peeled and deveined

Salt and freshly ground black pepper

SEARED HALIBUT

1 boneless, skinless halibut fillet (about 8 oz), cut crosswise into 4 pieces

1 Tbsp black sesame seeds

1 Tbsp white sesame seeds

2 Tbsp clarified butter (see page 177)

Since this dish features a trio of seafood—shrimp, trout, and halibut—and Keith (see page 64) reckons it's so good it's like sex on a plate, the name seems a natural. But, whatever you call it, it's a summertime feast. **SERVES 4**

PEPPERED TROUT GRAVLAX In a small bowl, stir together salt, pepper, and sugar. Lay trout fillets (skin side down) in a shallow dish large enough to hold them in a single layer. Sprinkle one-third of salt mixture evenly over trout. Arrange lemon slices and tarragon over top. Sprinkle with remaining salt mixture. Refrigerate, covered, for 10 hours. Remove trout from dish. Wipe all salt mixture off with paper towels. Just before serving, cut trout into very thin slices, cutting fish away from skin.

PICKLED FENNEL In a large saucepan, stir together fennel, wine, vinegar, sugar, salt, garlic, pepper, and bay leaf. Bring to a simmer over medium-high heat. Remove sauce-

pan from heat. Let cool to room temperature. (Pickled fennel may be refrigerated in an airtight container for up to 1 week, but bring to room temperature before serving.)

LEMON CHUTNEY In a medium saucepan, stir together onion, lemon juice, vinegar, and garlic. Bring to a boil over medium-high heat. Add leek and sugar. Reduce heat to medium-low, then simmer, uncovered, for 5–7 minutes or until leek is just tender (do not overcook).

In a small bowl, stir cornstarch with cold water until smooth. Add cornstarch mixture to saucepan. Simmer, stirring constantly, until mixture thickens slightly. Remove saucepan from the heat. Stir in basil, and salt and pepper to taste. Let cool slightly. Stir in lemon segments. Let cool to room temperature. (Lemon chutney may be refrigerated in an airtight container for up to 1 week, but bring to room temperature before serving.)

SAUTÉED SHRIMP In a medium skillet over medium heat, melt half of the butter. Add shallots. Cook for 8–10 minutes, stirring often, until shallots are soft and golden brown. Remove shallots with a slotted spoon. Set aside. Melt remaining butter in skillet. Add shrimp. Cook for 2–3 minutes, turning once, until shrimp are just pink and firm. Return shallots to skillet. Keep warm.

SEARED HALIBUT Remove any pin bones from halibut fillets with a pair of clean tweezers. Stir together white and black sesame seeds in a shallow dish. Coat halibut on all sides in sesame seed mixture. In a large skillet, heat clarified butter over medium-high heat. Add halibut. Cook for 6–8 minutes, turning once, until halibut is just cooked.

TO SERVE Put a halibut fillet on each of 4 plates. Add 2 shrimp and some trout gravlax to each plate. Garnish with pickled fennel and lemon chutney.

Fish, Seafood & Pasta

Kelly Attwells
HEAD CHEF

IN THE KITCHEN, KELLY SEEMS TO SCALE.
But one-on-one, when we're sitting at a normal table, his height becomes clearly constrained, his hands folded in front of him.

"My sense of baking came from spending time with my grandma. We always cooked.

"Travelling is my first passion. At 20 I went west to Seattle. I needed a job, so I picked up a dishwasher job. Everywhere I went, they needed a cook or a chef. Always.

"I learned by targeting restaurants I thought were the best and shadowing great chefs.

"My style is totally creative, no limitations. No schooling, I cook totally outside the box.

"My travelling helps. Cooking is complementary to my travelling. The food helps you understand a place and people. The food is part of a culture. It is a symbiotic relationship. And it's all about relationships. Travel, food, people.

"In recent years, I've become more concerned with where food comes from. We have a great relationship with Cincott Farms. They're great," he laughs, throwing his head back. "Even with the big suppliers, like Sysco, we can develop an awareness with them of where the food comes from. What's sustainable. What we want. They will meet our needs."

He stands, unwinding from the chair, "That's it? I better get up to the Lodge."

At ease again, he walks off.

Pan-Seared Miso Scallops
with Leek and Bacon

MISO DRESSING

3 Tbsp miso

1 egg yolk

1 cup light sesame oil

2 Tbsp canola oil

¼ cup mirin (Japanese sweet
   cooking wine)

3 Tbsp minced fresh ginger

MUSHROOM CAKES

3 Tbsp clarified butter
   (see page 177)

10 shallots, minced

4 cups finely diced fresh
   mushrooms (button, oyster,
   or shiitake)

2 cups dried wild mushrooms

2 eggs

½ cup mixture finely chopped
   fresh rosemary, thyme,
   and parsley

½ cup roasted garlic purée
   (see page 177)

Salt and freshly ground
   black pepper

APPLE TOPPING

5 slices smoked streaky bacon,
   finely diced

2 Yellow Delicious or Fuji
   apples, peeled, cored, and
   finely diced

1 leek (white part only),
   finely diced

PAN-SEARED SCALLOPS

12 Digby or other fresh
   large scallops

1 Tbsp canola oil

Salt and freshly ground
   white pepper

¼ cup finely chopped
   fresh chives

Pan-seared B.C. scallops, paired with apples from orchards near the Lodge and a Japanese miso dressing, blend the ocean and the mountain valleys with a touch of the Far East. Miso is a rich-tasting salty paste made from fermented soy beans, and is a mainstay of Japanese cuisine. Use white (shiro) miso for this recipe. Look for it in natural food stores or Asian grocery stores. Miso will keep indefinitely if refrigerated in an airtight container. **SERVES 4**

MISO DRESSING In food processor or blender, combine miso and egg yolk. Process until smooth. With processor running, gradually add sesame and canola oils in a thin stream until well combined. With processor still running, gradually add mirin until well combined. Add ginger and continue to process until dressing is creamy. Set aside.

MUSHROOM CAKES Preheat the oven to 350°F. Line a large baking sheet with parch-

ment paper. In a large skillet, heat butter over medium heat. Add shallots. Cook, stirring, for 3–5 minutes or until soft but not brown. Add fresh mushrooms. Cook, stirring often, for 8–10 minutes or until mushrooms are tender and mixture looks dry. Meanwhile, in a clean spice or coffee grinder, grind dried mushrooms in batches until they are ground to a fine powder.

In a food processor, process mushroom-shallot mixture until it forms a paste. Add

continued on page 76 . . .

Pan-Seared Miso Scallops with Leek and Bacon *(continued)*

ground dried mushrooms, eggs, rosemary-thyme-parsley mixture, garlic purée, and salt and pepper to taste. Process until well combined.

Spread mixture onto prepared baking sheet to form an 8-inch square cake, about 1 inch thick. Bake for 30–40 minutes until cake is set but remains slightly moist. Cut cake into 12 even-sized rectangles or rounds. Set aside and keep warm.

APPLE TOPPING In a large non-stick skillet, fry bacon over medium-high heat for 5–7 minutes or until crisp. Remove bacon with a slotted spoon and drain on a plate lined with paper towel. Drain off all but 1 Tbsp fat from skillet. Add apples to skillet. Cook over medium-high heat, stirring often, for 3–5 min-

utes or until apples are tender and caramelized. Stir in leek. Cook for 2–3 minutes or until just wilted. Return bacon to skillet. Set aside and keep warm.

PAN-SEARED SCALLOPS Remove the tough tendon on side of each scallop. Wash scallops well in cold water. Pat dry. In a large heavy skillet, heat oil over high heat. Sprinkle scallops with salt and pepper. Sear for about 1 minute on each side or until golden brown (do not overcook).

TO SERVE Arrange 3 mushroom cakes on each of 4 plates. Top each cake with 1 scallop. Spoon apple topping over scallops. Drizzle each plate with miso dressing. Garnish with chives.

Pan-Roasted Black Cod with Mussels and Black-Olive Gnocchi

BLACK-OLIVE GNOCCHI

6 large russet potatoes,
    scrubbed
Salt and freshly ground
    black pepper
½ cup good-quality kalamata
    olives, pitted and minced
2 egg yolks
Sifted all-purpose flour
    as needed

RED PEPPER PURÉE

4 roasted sweet red peppers
    (see page 177), coarsely
    chopped

CARAWAY BROWN BUTTER

1 cup butter
½ medium leek (white part
    only), finely diced
1 lemon
3 Tbsp toasted caraway seeds
Salt and freshly ground
    black pepper

PAN-ROASTED BLACK COD

4 black cod fillets (each
    about 8 oz)
Salt and freshly ground
    black pepper
2 Tbsp olive oil
12–16 mussels, in their shells
1 cup sake (Japanese rice wine)
1 Tbsp butter
¾ cup finely chopped parsley

Crunchy caraway seeds and smooth gnocchi (potato dumplings) add interesting flavour notes and contrasting textures to simple pan-roasted black cod (a.k.a. sablefish). **SERVES 4**

BLACK-OLIVE GNOCCHI Preheat the oven to 375°F. Sprinkle potatoes with salt and pepper. Bake, uncovered, for 1–1½ hours or until very tender. Spread olives out on a small baking sheet. Roast for 20–25 minutes or until olives are dry and powdery. Let cool then pulse in a food processor until finely ground.

While potatoes are still hot, cut them in half and scoop flesh from skins. Pass potato flesh through a food mill or rub through a fine sieve until smooth. Immediately, pile hot puréed potato in a volcano shape on a work surface (see photo next page). Dough must be prepared while potatoes are still warm. Make a "well" in the centre. Put olives, egg yolks, and more salt and pepper to taste into well.

Sift 1½–2 cups flour into well. Using a dough scraper, cut and fold ingredients together to form a stiff dough, adding more flour as necessary. Do not overmix dough or add too much flour.

Divide dough into quarters. Form each quarter into a 1-inch-diameter sausage. Cut sausages into 2-inch pieces. Roll tines of a fork over each piece of gnocchi to flatten it slightly. In a large pot of boiling salted water, cook gnocchi for about 3 minutes or until they float. Remove with a slotted spoon and place in a large bowl of ice water. Drain well. Spread gnocchi out in a single layer on a baking sheet. Refrigerate, loosely covered, until ready to serve.

continued on page 79 . . .

Pan-Roasted Black Cod with Mussels and Black-Olive Gnocchi *(continued)*

RED PEPPER PURÉE In a food processor, process peppers until smooth. Rub through a fine sieve. Set aside.

CARAWAY BROWN BUTTER In a small saucepan, melt 1 Tbsp butter over medium heat. Add leek. Cook, stirring, for 3–5 minutes or until soft but not browned. Add juice from lemon. In a separate small saucepan, combine remaining butter and caraway seeds. Cook over low heat until butter has melted, milk solids have separated, and butter starts to smell a little nutty. Stir in leek, lemon juice, and salt and pepper to taste. Remove from the heat and keep warm.

PAN-ROASTED BLACK COD Preheat the oven to 400°F. Sprinkle cod on both sides with salt and pepper to taste. In a large oven-proof skillet, heat 1 Tbsp oil over medium-high heat. Fry cod fillets for 2–3 minutes, turning once. Transfer skillet to the oven. Cook for 8–10 minutes more or until fish is just cooked.

Meanwhile, scrub mussels and trim off any beards with scissors. Discard any mussels that don't close when tapped sharply on the counter. In a medium saucepan, combine mussels, sake, and more salt and pepper to taste. Bring to a boil over high heat. Cook, covered, for about 5 minutes until mussels open (discard those that don't open). Drain mussels. Keep warm.

In a separate large skillet, heat butter and remaining oil over medium-high heat. Add gnocchi and parsley. Cook, stirring often, for 5–7 minutes until gnocchi are heated through.

TO SERVE Divide black-olive gnocchi among 4 plates. Top each portion with a piece of cod. Add 3 or 4 mussels to each plate. Drizzle cod and mussels with a little of the caraway brown butter. Garnish with red pepper purée.

Halibut Fillets with Warm Basil Olivada

BASIL OLIVADA
4 stalks celery, diced
1 small fennel bulb, trimmed
    and diced
1½ lemons
¾ cup olive oil
3 plum tomatoes, peeled,
    seeded, and diced

½ cup black olives, pitted
    and diced
2 Tbsp finely chopped fresh
    basil
Salt and freshly ground
    black pepper

HALIBUT
4 skinless halibut fillets
    (each about 6 oz)
1 Tbsp olive oil
Salt and freshly ground black
    pepper
Finely chopped fresh basil
    for garnish

*West coast halibut is enjoyed many different ways at the Lodge, including this easy grilled version.
Olivada is a cross between a vinaigrette and a sauce.* **SERVES 4**

BASIL OLIVADA Fill a medium saucepan with water, then bring to a boil over high heat. Add celery and fennel. Blanch for 1 minute. Drain and transfer vegetables to a bowl of ice water. Drain well.

Squeeze juice from lemons. In a medium saucepan, stir together lemon juice, celery, fennel, oil, tomatoes, olives, basil, and salt and pepper to taste. Set aside.

HALIBUT Preheat the barbecue to high. Brush halibut fillets with olive oil. Sprinkle with salt and pepper to taste. Grill halibut for 8–10 minutes, turning once, until just cooked. Meanwhile, gently heat basil olivada but do not boil.

TO SERVE Divide halibut fillets among 4 plates. Spoon olivada generously over each portion. Garnish with basil.

Potato-Crusted Halibut with Champagne Mayonnaise

CHAMPAGNE MAYONNAISE

1 egg yolk
1 Tbsp champagne vinegar
1 cup canola oil
Salt and freshly ground
   black pepper

ROASTED BUTTERNUT SQUASH PURÉE

1 medium shallot, peeled
1 tsp olive oil
1 medium butternut squash
¼ cup butter
1 medium sweet potato, peeled
   and cut into chunks

4 cloves garlic, unpeeled
¾ cup (approx.) whipping cream
Salt and freshly ground
   black pepper

BEURRE ROUGE

1 cup red wine
¼ cup red wine vinegar
2 Tbsp granulated sugar
1 medium shallot, cut into
   quarters
2 sprigs thyme
1 bay leaf
⅓ cup cold butter, cubed

Salt and freshly ground
   black pepper

POTATO-CRUSTED HALIBUT

4 skinless halibut fillets
   (each about 6 oz)
Salt and freshly ground
   black pepper
1 egg
1 Tbsp cold water
4 large russet potatoes, peeled
   and very thinly sliced
1 Tbsp canola oil
Finely chopped chives
   for garnish

Halibut encased in a crisp potato crust creates perfect comfort food for winter. For best results, use a mandoline slicer to cut the potatoes. SERVES 4

CHAMPAGNE MAYONNAISE In a blender, combine egg yolk and vinegar. Blend until smooth. With blender running, gradually add oil in a thin stream until mayonnaise is thickened and smooth. Season with salt and pepper to taste. Refrigerate until ready to serve.

ROASTED BUTTERNUT SQUASH PURÉE Preheat the oven to 350°F. In a small bowl, toss shallot with oil until well coated. Wrap loosely in foil. Roast for about 1 hour or until tender. When cool enough to handle, chop shallot finely. Set aside. Meanwhile, cut squash in half and remove seeds. Divide butter between hollows in each squash half (about 1 Tbsp in each). Roast squash cut sides up on a baking sheet lined with parchment paper for about 45 minutes or until tender.

In a medium saucepan, combine sweet potato with enough cold, salted water to cover it. Bring to a boil over high heat. Reduce heat to medium. Cook, covered, for 25–30 minutes or until tender. Drain well. Keep warm.

Meanwhile, in a small skillet over medium heat, toast garlic cloves for 5–7 minutes or until skins blacken and garlic cloves soften. Remove from the skillet. Let cool slightly. Pop garlic out of skins, then mince finely.

Scoop flesh from squash. In a food processor, combine squash, sweet potato, roasted garlic, shallot, and remaining butter. Process until smooth. In a small saucepan, heat cream until steaming. Add about ½ cup cream to food processor. Process until smooth and creamy, adding more cream as necessary (you may not need it all). Season with salt and pepper to taste. Keep warm.

continued on next page . . .

Potato-Crusted Halibut with Champagne Mayonnaise *(continued)*

BEURRE ROUGE In a medium saucepan, stir together red wine, vinegar, sugar, shallot, thyme, and bay leaf. Bring to a boil over high heat. Reduce heat to medium and continue to boil until liquid reduces to about ½ cup. Strain, discarding solids. Return liquid to saucepan over low heat. Gradually whisk in butter 1 piece at a time, allowing each piece of butter to melt before adding more. Season with salt and pepper to taste. Keep warm over very low heat.

POTATO-CRUSTED HALIBUT Preheat the oven to 400°F. Line a large baking sheet with parchment paper. Sprinkle fish with salt and pepper to taste. In a small bowl, beat egg with cold water. Brush top side of each piece of fish with egg mixture. Arrange potato slices in overlapping rows on eggy side of each piece of fish to resemble fish scales.

In a large non-stick skillet, heat oil over medium-high heat. Add fish, potato side down, and cook, without moving the fish, for 3–5 minutes or until potatoes are golden. Carefully transfer fish, potato side up, to prepared baking sheet. Roast for 8–10 minutes or until fish is just cooked and potatoes are tender.

TO SERVE Spoon roasted butternut squash purée onto 4 plates. Centre the halibut on the purée. Drizzle fish with beurre rouge. Garnish with champagne mayonnaise and chives.

Salmon Fillets in White Wine and Thyme Sauce

1 large leek (white part only),
   cut into matchstick strips
½ lemon
¾ cup dry white wine
2 shallots, minced
3 cloves garlic, thinly sliced

1 sprig thyme
5 Tbsp cold butter, cubed
1 large tomato, peeled, seeded,
   and diced
Salt and freshly ground
   black pepper

4 skinless wild salmon fillets
   (each about 4 oz)
Thyme sprigs for garnish

Salmon—Alain's favourites are sockeye and coho—is the quintessential B.C. dish, and carries so much flavour it needs only steamed seasonal vegetables as an accompaniment. **SERVES 4**

Preheat the oven to 250°F. In a small saucepan of boiling water, blanch leek for 2 minutes. Drain, then transfer to bowl of ice water to cool. Drain well. Put leek in a small ovenproof dish in oven.

Squeeze juice from lemon half. In a small non-reactive saucepan, combine lemon juice, wine, shallots, and garlic. Strip leaves from thyme sprig and add leaves to saucepan. Bring to a simmer over medium heat. Simmer for 5 minutes or until flavours are blended. Reduce heat to low. Gradually whisk in 4 Tbsp butter 1 piece at a time, allowing each piece of butter to melt before adding more. Stir in tomato, and salt and pepper to taste. Keep warm over very low heat.

Meanwhile, in a large heavy skillet, heat remaining butter over high heat. Sprinkle salmon with more salt and pepper to taste. Cook for 6–8 minutes, turning once, until just cooked but still coral-coloured in the centre.

Divide leek among 4 plates. Top each portion with a piece of salmon. Spoon sauce over salmon. Garnish with thyme.

Fish, Seafood & Pasta

Alain Stahl
Alain Stahl
FIRST LODGE CHEF

WHENEVER YOU MENTION THE EARLY DAYS of Island Lake Lodge, Alain's name always comes up. And that of his dog, Cashew.

With the first lodge built on the property, Dan MacDonald needed a chef. After landing in Quebec, Alain spent two and a half years slowly moving west, and landed in Fernie as Dan started looking for a chef. Growing up in Marlecheim Alsace, his approach was decidedly French. The province is relatively rural and Alain appreciated the honest flavours of free-range and organic produce long before they brecame trendy.

"I grew up on a farm and so could easily apply what I knew out here."

With training in Michelin Two Star restaurants, he brought a formal structure to the kitchen, tempered by a love of innovation.

"The Lodge was really a mom-and-pop operation when I first started. Cashew and I lived upstairs in the Bear.

"In the morning, I'd walk downstairs and start cooking. I try to find true flavours. Organic and free-range are best. With free-range chicken, it's so good you really don't have to do much.

"Between the first and the second year, we built the second lodge. I built all the beds and furniture. It got me going and thinking." After eight years, Alain moved out of the kitchen into a woodshop. "Eventually I left and started Bisaro Woodworks. I still build all the Lodge furniture."

More than that, Alain firmly established the ethic of using organic, free-range produce, and established the structure of sous chef moving to head chef that exists at the Lodge to this day.

Halibut Baked with a Parsley Crust

CREAMY MASHED POTATOES

4 large Kennebec or baking
    potatoes, peeled and cut
    into chunks
⅔ cup 10% cream
6 Tbsp butter
3 cloves garlic, peeled
3 sprigs thyme
1 bay leaf
Salt and freshly ground
    white pepper

HORSERADISH CREAM

2 tsp butter
2 cloves garlic, thinly sliced
1 shallot, minced
½ cup dry white wine
2–3 Tbsp prepared horseradish,
    to taste
1 cup whipping cream
Liquid honey to taste
Salt and freshly ground
    white pepper
1 plum tomato, peeled, seeded,
    and diced

BAKED HALIBUT

1–1½ cups panko breadcrumbs
1 bunch parsley, washed and
    stems removed
2 Tbsp butter, melted
4 skinless halibut fillets
    (each about 4 oz)
Salt and freshly ground
    white pepper

On a cold winter night, serve this hearty dish with broccolini (pictured), green beans, or spinach, to give you energy for yet another day on the mountain. Panko are Japanese breadcrumbs; look for them in specialty stores or major supermarkets. **SERVES 4**

CREAMY MASHED POTATOES Put potatoes in a large saucepan with enough cold, salted water to cover them. Bring to a boil over high heat. Reduce heat to medium-low, then simmer, covered, for about 20 minutes or until tender. Meanwhile, in a small saucepan, combine cream, butter, garlic, thyme, and bay leaf and simmer over medium-low heat for 10 minutes. Strain hot cream, discarding solids. Keep warm.

Drain potatoes. Pass through a food mill or rub through a fine sieve until smooth. Stir in cream, and salt and pepper to taste. Keep warm.

HORSERADISH CREAM In a small heavy saucepan, melt butter over medium heat. Add garlic and shallots. Cook for 3–5 minutes, stirring often, until soft but not brown. Add wine. Bring to a boil over medium-high heat. Add horseradish. Simmer until liquid reduces by about half. Add cream and continue to simmer until sauce is thick enough to coat the back of a spoon. Season with honey and salt and pepper to taste. Set aside. Keep warm. Just before serving, stir in tomato.

BAKED HALIBUT In a food processor, process panko breadcrumbs until very finely ground. Add parsley. Continue processing until very finely minced. Add butter and continue processing until well combined. Tip crumb mixture onto a large sheet of parchment paper. Top with a second sheet of paper. Roll out crumb mixture between paper until it is about ¼ inch thick. Slide paper and crumb mixture onto a large baking sheet. Freeze for 10 minutes or until set.

Preheat the oven to 400°F. Line a large baking sheet with parchment paper. Sprinkle fish on both sides with salt and pepper to taste. Remove crumb mixture from freezer. Peel off top layer of paper. With a sharp knife, carefully cut 4 pieces of crumb mixture the same size as each piece of fish. Top each piece of fish with a piece of crumb mixture. Put the crumb-topped fish on prepared baking sheet. Bake for 10–12 minutes, depending on thickness, until fish is just cooked.

TO SERVE Divide mashed potatoes among 4 plates. Top with halibut and drizzle with horseradish cream. Serve with steamed broccolini or other greens.

Smoked Salmon Napoleon

BRINE

2 cups apple cider

¾ cup Japanese soy sauce

4 Tbsp coriander seeds, toasted
   and ground

2 Tbsp coarse salt

½ cup water

1 salmon fillet (about 1 lb;
   preferably coho)

Cedar, hickory, or apple
   wood chips

MANGO SALAD

2 unripe mangoes

2 cups dry white wine

½ cup granulated sugar

⅓ cup slivered fresh Thai
   or Italian basil

SUSHI RICE

1 cup Japanese short-grain rice

1 cup water

1 strip kombu (optional)

6 Tbsp rice vinegar

5 Tbsp granulated sugar

1 Tbsp coarse salt

2 Tbsp canola oil

GARNISH

1 lemon

1 firm, ripe avocado

¼ cup Japanese soy sauce

3 Tbsp sake (Japanese
   rice wine)

2 Tbsp liquid honey

Sweet potato chips for garnish

Shredded daikon (Japanese
   radish) for garnish

East meets west in this house-smoked salmon served with avocado, mango, and sushi rice. Kombu is Japanese sun-dried seaweed. Find it in natural food stores or Asian grocery stores. SERVES 4

BRINE In a non-reactive dish large enough to hold salmon, stir together cider, soy sauce, coriander seeds, salt, and water. Add salmon to dish, making sure it's submerged in brine. Refrigerate, covered, overnight.

Remove salmon from brine. Place on rack set over a rimmed baking sheet. Let stand at room temperature for 1 hour or until salmon secretes a jelly-like substance.

Smoke salmon in a smoker or on a barbecue, using wood chips, for 45–60 minutes or until fish flakes easily but is not dry, or follow manufacturer's instructions. Let salmon cool. Refrigerate until ready to serve.

MANGO SALAD Using a vegetable peeler, peel mangoes. Use peeler to cut thin ribbons from mangoes, discarding pits. In a medium saucepan, combine mangoes, wine, and sugar. Bring to a boil over medium-high heat. Reduce heat to medium-low, then simmer, stirring occasionally, until mango is tender and most of liquid has evaporated. Remove from the heat. Let cool completely. Stir in basil.

SUSHI RICE In a medium bowl, combine rice with enough cold water to cover it. Gently swirl rice until water becomes milky. Drain. Repeat process 3 or 4 times of until water is almost clear. Tip rice into a sieve. Let stand for 30 minutes. In a rice cooker or medium saucepan, combine rice and water. Let stand for 45 minutes. Add kombu, if using. Cook rice according to rice-cooker manufacturer's instructions. If using a saucepan, bring rice and water to a boil over high heat. Reduce heat to low. Cook, covered, for 25 minutes or until rice is tender and liquid is absorbed. Remove from the heat. Fluff rice with a fork. Let stand for 10 minutes.

Meanwhile, in a small saucepan, stir together vinegar, sugar, and salt. Heat over medium heat, stirring until sugar and salt have dissolved. Remove from the heat. Let cool completely.

Spread rice out in a shallow non-reactive dish. Sprinkle with vinegar mixture. Stir to combine. Spread out and let cool to room temperature. Form rice into ¾-inch squares. In a large non-stick skillet, heat canola oil over medium-high heat. Add rice squares. Cook, turning often, until golden on all sides.

GARNISH Squeeze juice from lemon. Put 1 tsp lemon juice in a medium bowl. Peel, pit, and thinly slice avocado into bowl. Toss with lemon juice. Set aside.

In a small saucepan, stir together remaining lemon juice, the soy sauce, sake, and honey. Heat over medium-low heat until honey dissolves. Set aside.

TO SERVE Cut salmon into thin diagonal slices. Divide sushi-rice squares among 4 plates. Top first with salmon, then avocado, then mango salad. Garnish with sweet potato chips and shredded daikon.

Dark Rye–Dusted West Coast Salmon

POTATO LATKES
½ lb Kennebec or baking
  potatoes, peeled and
  shredded
2 large stalks celery, shredded
¼ cup finely chopped parsley
Salt and freshly ground black
  pepper
½ cup clarified butter
  (see page 177)

TARRAGON BUTTER
½ cup butter, softened

¼ cup finely chopped
  fresh tarragon
Salt and freshly ground
  black pepper

BRAISED SPINACH
½ cup chicken stock
  (see page 176)
1 small onion, finely diced
6 cups baby spinach
1 roasted red pepper
  (see page 176), cut into
  matchstick strips

1 Tbsp butter
Salt and freshly ground
  black pepper

SALMON
½ cup dark rye flour
Salt and freshly ground
  black pepper
4 wild coho salmon fillets
  (each about 6 oz)
½ cup extra virgin canola oil
Tarragon sprigs for garnish

The contrast of dark rye flour against the bright coral colour of the salmon makes this a stunning dish. SERVES 4

POTATO LATKES In a large bowl, stir together potato, celery, parsley, and salt and pepper to taste. Form mixture into 4 patties. In a large non-stick skillet, heat butter over medium-high heat. Add potato latkes. Fry for 3–5 minutes, turning once, until just golden. Remove from skillet. Refrigerate, covered, until ready to serve.

TARRAGON BUTTER Using an electric mixer, beat butter until smooth in a small bowl. Add tarragon, and salt and pepper to taste. Beat until well combined. Refrigerate for at least 1 hour or until firm.

BRAISED SPINACH In a medium saucepan, stir together stock and onion. Bring to a boil over medium-high heat. Reduce heat to medium-low, then simmer, uncovered, until onion is tender. Stir in spinach, roasted pepper, butter, and salt and pepper to taste. Cook over low heat just until spinach wilts. Remove from the heat. Keep warm.

SALMON Preheat the oven to 400°F. Put latkes on a baking sheet lined with parchment paper and reheat in oven. In a shallow dish, stir together rye flour, and salt and pepper to taste. Dip salmon fillets in flour to coat completely. In a large ovenproof skillet, heat oil over medium-high heat. Add salmon to skillet. Cook for about 2 minutes on each side. Transfer skillet to the oven. Cook for another 5–7 minutes until salmon is just cooked yet remains coral-coloured in the centre.

TO SERVE Divide braised spinach among 4 shallow bowls. Put a salmon fillet alongside each portion of spinach. Lean a potato latke against each portion of spinach. Top each salmon fillet with tarragon butter. Garnish with tarragon.

Island Lake Lodge Fresh Fettuccine

PASTA
10 egg yolks
2 eggs
2 Tbsp olive oil
2 Tbsp milk
3 cups sifted all-purpose flour,
   plus extra for dredging

TO FINISH
2 lb heirloom tomatoes,
   diced or quartered depending
   on size
1½ cups grated Parmesan
   cheese

1 bunch basil, coarsely chopped
   and stems removed
Salt and freshly ground
   black pepper
⅓ cup olive oil
Shaved Parmesan cheese
   to serve

When the tomatoes at Cincott Farms (see page 57) come into season, this signature dish is a favourite served on the deck overlooking the lake. For best flavour, use good-quality Parmigiano-Reggiano cheese. The pasta recipe makes more dough than you'll need. Form the dough into three balls, and wrap and freeze two for later use. **SERVES 4**

PASTA Using a stand mixer fitted with a dough hook, beat egg yolks, eggs, oil, and milk until well combined. With mixer running on low speed, gradually add flour, ½ cup at a time, until all incorporated. Knead dough in mixer for 15 minutes. (It's impossible to over-knead the dough, more kneading creates a silkier pasta.) Form dough into 3 balls. Wrap 2 balls in plastic wrap and freeze for later use. Let remaining dough rest at room temperature for 1 hour.

Cut ball of dough into thirds. Flatten each third with the palm of your hand and form into a rectangular shape. Roll out each section to about ⅛ inch thick, roll up and cut with a knife (see photo left). Or, using a pasta machine adjusted to its widest setting,

pass each piece of dough through machine. Gradually reduce setting to finest or second finest, according to your preference. Use the cutting attachment to cut pasta into fettuccine noodles. Dredge noodles with more flour. Hang to dry for about 2 hours.

TO FINISH In a large pot of boiling, salted water, cook fettuccine for 5–7 minutes or until al dente. Meanwhile, in a large warm serving bowl, combine tomatoes, Parmesan cheese, basil, and salt and pepper taste. In a small skillet, heat oil over medium-high heat.

TO SERVE Drain pasta. Add to tomato mixture, along with oil. Toss well to combine. Serve at once with shaved Parmesan cheese.

Poultry & Meat

Chicken Breast Provençal

RED PEPPER COULIS
2 red peppers, halved
   and seeded
2 shallots, coarsely chopped
3 cloves garlic, minced
1 Tbsp olive oil
¾ cup dry white wine
¾ cup chicken stock
   (see page 176) or water

CHICKEN
¼ cup sliced almonds
¼ cup fresh breadcrumbs
4 cloves garlic, coarsely
   chopped
1 cup lightly packed parsley
   leaves (no stems)
2 Tbsp olive oil

Salt and freshly ground
   black pepper
4 free-range boneless chicken
   breasts with skin
1 Tbsp Dijon mustard
1 Tbsp butter
1 tsp red wine vinegar
Finely chopped parsley
   for garnish

In rural Alsace where Alain grew up, the only chickens his family cooked ran free on their farm. Today, the Lodge's chefs still seek out free-range, and preferably organically raised, chicken. This dish pairs well with creamy polenta or a mushroom risotto. **SERVES 4**

RED PEPPER COULIS Preheat the oven to 400°F. In a shallow roasting pan, toss together peppers, shallots, garlic, and oil. Roast, uncovered, for 20 minutes or until peppers and shallots are tender but not browned. Transfer peppers to a medium bowl. Cover tightly with plastic wrap. Set aside for 10 minutes. When cool enough to handle, remove skin and stems from peppers.

In a medium saucepan, combine peppers, shallots, garlic, and wine. Bring to a boil over medium-high heat. Reduce heat to medium, then simmer for 5 minutes. Add stock. Simmer for 5 more minutes. Remove saucepan from the heat. Let cool for a few minutes. In a food processor, process pepper mixture until smooth. Strain through a fine sieve back into same saucepan. Set aside.

CHICKEN Preheat the oven to 400°F. In a food processor, combine almonds, breadcrumbs, and garlic, then process until chopped. Add parsley to almond mixture, then process just until minced. Scrape down sides of processor with a rubber spatula. Add 1 Tbsp oil, and salt and pepper to taste. Process just until combined. Scrape almond mixture into a bowl.

In a large ovenproof skillet, heat remaining oil over medium-high heat. Sprinkle chicken breasts with more salt and pepper to taste. Cook chicken breasts for 2 minutes on each side or until golden. Remove skillet from the heat. Spread top of each chicken breast with mustard. Spread almond mixture on top of chicken breasts, dividing evenly and pressing it firmly so that it adheres. Transfer skillet to oven. Roast for 10 minutes or until a meat thermometer inserted into thickest chicken breast registers 160°F, and chicken is no longer pink inside.

Meanwhile, heat red pepper coulis over medium-low heat until simmering. Whisk in butter and vinegar. Season with more salt and pepper to taste.

TO SERVE Slice each chicken breast, then fan out slices on each of 4 plates, dividing evenly. Drizzle chicken with red pepper coulis. Garnish with parsley.

Butter Curry Free-Range Chicken

BUTTER CURRY CHICKEN
1 cup clarified butter
  (see page 177)
1 onion, finely diced
2 Tbsp minced garlic
2 Tbsp minced fresh ginger
2 Tbsp cumin seeds, toasted
  and ground
2 Tbsp turmeric
1 Tbsp coriander seeds, toasted
  and ground
1 Tbsp curry powder
Cinnamon to taste

1 Tbsp sambal oelek
  (Indonesian hot sauce)
1 can (5½ oz) tomato paste
2 cups whipping cream
1 Tbsp liquid honey
1 large lemon
4–6 fresh free-range bone-in,
  skin-on chicken legs (thighs
  attached)
Salt and freshly ground
  black pepper
2 Tbsp canola oil

**COCONUT-LIME
BASMATI RICE**
1 cup basmati rice
1½ cups water
2 limes
½ cup unsweetened desiccated
  coconut
Salt and freshly ground
  black pepper
Grated lime zest for garnish

Free-range chicken is more flavourful than factory-raised chicken. Here, it's slow-cooked butter-curry style, and served with coconut-lime basmati rice. **SERVES 4**

BUTTER CURRY CHICKEN In a large oven-proof casserole, heat butter over medium heat. Add onion. Cook, stirring, for 3–5 minutes or until softened but not browned. Add garlic and ginger. Cook, stirring, for 1 minute.

Meanwhile, in a small skillet over medium heat, toast ground cumin, turmeric, coriander, curry powder, and cinnamon for 1–2 minutes or until fragrant. Add half of the cumin mixture and the sambal oelek to the onion mixture. Cook, stirring, for 1–2 minutes. Stir in tomato paste. Cook, stirring, for 3–5 minutes or until mixture thickens slightly. Gradually whisk in cream and honey. Squeeze in juice from lemon. Drop lemon halves into sauce. Reduce heat to low, then simmer, uncovered, for 10 minutes.

Preheat the oven to 325°F. Cut around the circumference of the thinnest end of each leg to release the skin and tendons. Sprinkle chicken with salt and pepper to taste. Dust with remaining cumin mixture. In a large heavy skillet, heat oil over medium-high heat. Cook chicken for 5–7 minutes or until golden brown on both sides. Add chicken to curry

sauce. Transfer casserole to oven. Bake, covered, for 2 hours or until chicken is tender and no longer pink inside.

COCONUT-LIME BASMATI RICE In a medium bowl, combine rice with enough cold water to cover. Gently swirl rice until water becomes milky. Drain. Repeat process 3 or 4 times of until water is almost clear. In a medium saucepan, combine drained rice and water. Set aside to soak for 20 minutes, then bring to a boil over medium-high heat. Reduce heat to low, then cook, covered, for 20–25 minutes or until rice is tender and liquid absorbed. Fluff rice with a fork.

Meanwhile, squeeze juice from limes. In a large non-stick skillet, stir together lime juice, coconut, and salt and pepper to taste. Toast over medium heat until golden, stirring often so coconut cooks evenly but does not burn. Stir coconut mixture into rice.

TO SERVE Divide coconut-lime basmati rice among 4 plates. Top with chicken and butter curry sauce. Garnish with lime zest.

Chicken Supreme with Tomato Hollandaise

CHICKEN

¼ cup olive oil
1 Tbsp finely chopped parsley
1 Tbsp finely chopped fresh
    oregano
1 Tbsp finely chopped fresh
    thyme
1 Tbsp finely chopped fresh
    rosemary
4 free-range boneless chicken
    breasts with skin
2 Tbsp canola oil
Salt and freshly ground black
    pepper

LENTILS

1 cup Puy lentils
1 large carrot, peeled
    and quartered
1 onion, quartered
1 stalk celery, cut in half
2 cloves garlic, peeled
4 sprigs parsley
2 Tbsp olive oil
2 shallots, minced
⅓ cup fresh green peas,
    blanched
¼ cup chicken stock
    (see page 176)
Salt and freshly ground
    black pepper
¼ cup peeled, seeded,
    and diced tomato
1 Tbsp finely chopped parsley

TOMATO HOLLANDAISE

¼ cup water
3 Tbsp white wine vinegar
3 Tbsp fresh lemon juice
1 shallot, coarsely chopped
1 clove garlic, coarsely chopped
3 sprigs thyme
10 peppercorns
3 egg yolks
1 cup clarified butter
    (see page 177) at room
    temperature
4 plum tomatoes, peeled,
    seeded, and diced
1 tsp tomato paste
Pinch cayenne pepper
Salt and freshly ground black
    pepper
Parsley, oregano, thyme, or
    rosemary sprigs for garnish

This simple dish is a favourite menu item at the Lodge during the winter months. To add variety, the kitchen switches the sauce from this classic French tomato-spiked hollandaise (the more posh name is sauce choron*) to a* maltaise *(with blood orange juice and zest), or Béarnaise (with tarragon). Puy lentils are small, dark green lentils from France.* **SERVES 4**

CHICKEN In a shallow dish large enough to hold the chicken in a single layer, stir together olive oil, parsley, oregano, thyme, and rosemary. Add chicken, turning to coat well with herb mixture. Let stand at room temperature for 45 minutes. Preheat the oven to 400°F.

In a large ovenproof skillet, heat canola oil over medium-high heat. Sprinkle chicken breasts with salt and pepper to taste. Add to skillet. Cook for 3–5 minutes, turning once, until golden. Turn chicken breasts skin side up. Transfer skillet to oven. Roast for about 10 minutes or until a meat thermometer inserted into thickest chicken breast registers 160°F, and chicken is no longer pink inside.

LENTILS In a large saucepan, combine lentils, carrot, onion, celery, garlic, parsley sprigs, and 4 cups water. Bring to a boil over high heat. Reduce heat to medium-low. Simmer, covered, for about 40 minutes or until lentils are tender. (Do not overcook.) Drain, and remove and discard carrot, onion, celery, garlic, and parsley sprigs.

continued on page 106 ...

Chicken Supreme with Tomato Hollandaise *(continued)*

In a large skillet, heat oil over medium heat. Add shallots. Cook, stirring, for 3–5 minutes or until soft but not brown. Stir in lentils, peas, chicken stock, and salt and pepper to taste. Cook, stirring, for 5–7 minutes or until heated through. Stir in tomato and chopped parsley. Keep warm.

TOMATO HOLLANDAISE In a small saucepan, stir together water, vinegar, lemon juice, shallot, garlic, thyme, and peppercorns. Bring to a boil over medium heat. Boil until liquid reduces by half. Strain through a fine sieve, discarding solids. Let vinegar mixture cool slightly.

In a heatproof bowl set over a saucepan of simmering water, whisk together vinegar mixture and egg yolks. Whisking constantly, cook until the whisk leaves a trail and mixture is light and fluffy. Remove bowl from the heat. Continue whisking constantly while adding the clarified butter in a thin stream until well combined. Stir in tomatoes, tomato paste, cayenne, and salt and pepper to taste.

TO SERVE Divide chicken among 4 plates. Spoon lentils alongside. Drizzle with tomato hollandaise. Garnish with fresh herbs.

Smoked Duck Breast with Saskatoon Berry Salad

BRINE

1 cup Japanese soy sauce
2 cups apple cider
½ cup dark sesame oil

DUCK

4 whole duck breasts
Brine (recipe above)
2 cups alder wood chips

TOASTED BARLEY

2 cups chicken stock
  (see page 176)
¾ cup pearl barley
1 Tbsp butter

1 small sweet red pepper,
  seeded and finely diced
1 medium shallot, minced
¼ cup peeled, seeded,
  and diced tomato
1 Tbsp finely chopped parsley
Salt and freshly ground
  black pepper

BÉCHAMEL SAUCE

1 cup milk
1 onion, coarsely chopped
¼ cup maple syrup
Pinch grated nutmeg
2 Tbsp butter
2 Tbsp all-purpose flour

4 oz Oka cheese, shredded
Salt and freshly ground
  black pepper

SASKATOON BERRY SALAD

½ cup olive oil
¼ cup red wine vinegar
½ cup saskatoon berries
Salt and freshly ground black
  pepper
4 cups mixed greens

TO FINISH

1 Tbsp canola oil
Salt and freshly ground black
  pepper

Rich-tasting, smoked duck breasts require something acidic to balance the flavours. Saskatoons in the salad do the job beautifully. Saskatoons are wild berries from the Prairies that are similar to blueberries. Feel free to substitute blueberries if saskatoons are not available. **SERVES 4**

BRINE Combine soy sauce, apple cider and sesame oil in a large bowl. Set aside.

DUCK Trim off any excess fat from edges of duck breasts. With a sharp knife, score skin and fat of each breast in a crosshatch pattern. Put duck breasts in a shallow dish large enough to hold them in a single layer. Pour brine over duck breasts, making sure they are completely submerged in brine. Refrigerate, covered, for 12 hours. Remove duck breasts from brine. Smoke duck breasts in a smoker or on a barbecue, with alder wood chips, for 3 hours or until flavour is infused but the breasts remain uncooked, or follow manufacturer's instructions. Let cool. Refrigerate, covered, until ready to serve.

TOASTED BARLEY In a medium saucepan, combine stock and barley. Bring to a boil over high heat. Reduce heat to medium-low, then simmer, covered, for 45 minutes or until barley is tender. Drain well.

In a medium skillet, melt butter over medium-high heat. Add pepper and shallot. Cook, stirring, for 5–7 minutes or until soft but not brown. Stir in barley, tomato, parsley, and salt and pepper to taste. Set aside.

BÉCHAMEL SAUCE In a small saucepan, stir together milk, onion, maple syrup, and nutmeg over medium-low heat. Cook until just simmering. Reduce heat to low and continue to simmer, partially covered, for 25 minutes or until flavours are blended. Strain milk through a fine sieve, discarding onion.

continued on next page . . .

Smoked Duck Breast with Saskatoon Berry Salad *(continued)*

In a medium saucepan, melt butter over medium heat. Add flour. Cook, stirring, for 1–2 minutes or until mixture looks dry. Gradually whisk in milk until mixture becomes smooth. Cook, whisking constantly, until sauce bubbles and thickens. Remove from the heat. Stir in cheese until melted. Taste and add salt and pepper if necessary. Set aside.

SASKATOON BERRY SALAD In a medium bowl, whisk together oil and vinegar until creamy. Stir in saskatoon berries, and salt and pepper to taste. Just before serving, add frisée to dressing. Toss well.

TO FINISH Preheat the oven to 400°F. Heat a large heavy ovenproof skillet over medium-high heat, then add oil. Sprinkle duck breasts with salt and pepper to taste. Place duck breasts fat side down in skillet. Cook for

30 seconds. Reduce heat to low. Cook for 3–5 minutes or until some of the fat is rendered, basting breasts with the juices in the skillet. Pour excess fat from skillet. Transfer skillet to oven. Cook for 5–7 minutes or until a meat thermometer inserted into thickest breast registers 120°F for rare. Remove breasts to a cutting board. Tent loosely with foil and let rest for 5 minutes.

TO SERVE Reheat béchamel sauce and toasted barley. Slice duck breasts. Fan out slices on each of 4 plates. Spoon toasted barley alongside. Drizzle duck with béchamel sauce. Serve with saskatoon berry salad.

The Ten-Kilometre Beef

AS YOU HEAD west out of Fernie on Highway 3, you cross a bridge over the Elk River. After a couple of kilometres you reach Island Lake Road. At this junction lies a small ranch. A large traditional gambrel barn and two smaller barns sit against the rise of the river bench. Behind the barns, overlooking the broad hay field between the barns and the highway, is a small ranch house. This is the ranch and home of Fred Vandenberghe, a long-time valley resident, who helps his grandkids raise 4-H Champion beef. This ranch could just as well be called the Island Lake Beef Farm.

On a warm summer day a couple weeks before the annual 4-H auction, head chef Kelly Attwells drops in to see the beef on the hoof before the auction.

Running his hand down the flank of his grandson Sean's Angus, Fred explains, "We only feed them grain and grass. It's all natural. This one will be a Grand Champion for Sean again. The second year in a row." He runs his hand down the flank again. "Look at the depth on him here. And see how wide he is? Nice."

Fred moves over to Sarah and Tyson's beeves and repeats the motions. "We always have fine marbling in the beef."

At the 4-H auction, Sean indeed took home a second Grand Champion ribbon, and Island Lake Lodge won the bid for the beef. All the proceeds went to Sean, as the 4-H member raising the beef.

And next year, around the same time, there will be another three huge Angus standing in Fred's field getting the once-over.

Cherry Jus–Braised Organic Beef Short Ribs

BRAISED SHORT RIBS

16 cups beef stock
  (see page 176)
2 lb sweet black cherries
¼ cup balsamic syrup
  (see page 177)
¼ cup red wine syrup
  (see page 177)
½ cup thyme sprigs, tied
  in cheesecloth
6 organic beef short ribs
  (about 2½ lb)
Salt and freshly ground
  black pepper
¼ cup (approx.) canola oil

TOASTED SESAME SAUCE

2 cups sesame seeds
⅓ cup fresh orange juice
¼ cup roasted garlic purée
  (see page 177)
¼ cup minced fresh ginger
¼ cup soy sauce
3 Tbsp grated orange zest
3 Tbsp liquid honey
2 Tbsp mayonnaise
1¼ Tbsp sesame oil

SWEET POTATO TEMPURA

1 cup all-purpose flour
1 cup ice water
4 ice cubes
1 egg yolk
Canola oil for deep-frying
2 sweet potatoes, peeled and
  cut into ¼-inch slices
Additional all-purpose flour
  for dredging

The Lodge is proud to serve organic beef raised at a farm just at the bottom of the road (see page 113). Here, a rich braise of short ribs is paired with toasted sesame sauce and crispy sweet-potato tempura. Serve with wilted spinach or your favourite vegetable. SERVES 4

BRAISED SHORT RIBS In a large pot, bring beef stock to a boil over high heat. Boil until stock reduces to 8 cups. Set aside.

Meanwhile, preheat the oven to 400°F. Spread cherries out on a large rimmed baking sheet. Roast for 10 minutes to intensify their flavour and make pits easier to remove. When cherries cool enough to handle, remove pits. In a food processor, process cherries until a smooth purée forms. Reduce oven temperature to 275°F.

In a large ovenproof casserole, combine reduced stock, cherry purée, and balsamic and red wine syrups. Add cheesecloth bag of thyme. Bring to a boil over high heat. Reduce heat to medium-low, then simmer, uncovered, while you prepare the short ribs.

Sprinkle ribs with salt and pepper to taste. Heat a large heavy skillet over medium-high heat, then add 2 Tbsp oil. Cook ribs in batches for 3–5 minutes or until browned on all sides, removing ribs to casserole as each batch browns. Add more oil to skillet as necessary. Bring contents of casserole to a boil over high heat. Transfer casserole to oven. Cook, covered, for 6 hours or until meat is very tender and falling from bones.

Remove short ribs from braising liquid. Keep warm. Strain braising liquid through a sieve lined with cheesecloth. Return liquid to casserole. Boil liquid over high heat until it reduces and is slightly thickened. Keep warm over low heat.

TOASTED SESAME SAUCE In a medium skillet over medium heat, toast sesame seeds until seeds are dark golden and their oil begins to sweat out. Remove from the heat. Let cool completely. In a clean spice or coffee grinder, grind sesame seeds to a fine powder.

continued on page 116 . . .

Cherry Jus–Braised Organic Beef Short Ribs *(continued)*

In a medium bowl, stir together sesame-seed powder, orange juice, garlic purée, ginger, soy sauce, orange zest, honey, mayonnaise, and sesame oil. Set aside.

SWEET POTATO TEMPURA Put flour in a medium stainless-steel bowl. Place bowl of flour and a pair of chopsticks in the freezer for 45 minutes. Remove bowl and chopsticks. Add ice water, ice cubes, and egg yolk to flour. Lightly mix batter with chopsticks. Do not overmix (batter should remain lumpy).

Just before serving, pour oil into a large skillet to a depth of 2 inches. Heat over high heat until a candy thermometer registers 350°F. Dredge sweet potato slices in flour.

Dip in batter, coating completely and shaking to remove excess. Fry sweet potato in small batches for 2–3 minutes or until golden and crisp. Remove each batch with a slotted spoon and transfer to plate lined with paper towel. Keep warm.

TO SERVE Spoon a pool of reduced braising liquid on each of 4 plates. Divide ribs among plates, arranging them on braising liquid. Warm toasted sesame sauce slightly. Stack sweet potato tempura alongside ribs on each plate. Garnish with a drizzle of sauce.

Veal Saltimbocca with Carrot-Parsnip Terrine

CARROT-PARSNIP TERRINE
6 carrots, coarsely chopped
4 parsnips, coarsely chopped
3 sprigs thyme
1 bay leaf
2 Tbsp butter
3 eggs
⅓ cup whipping cream
Salt and freshly ground white
    pepper
Additional butter for greasing

VEAL
8 thin veal cutlets (each about
    2½ oz)
1 Tbsp Dijon mustard
1 Tbsp liquid honey
4 thin slices prosciutto
12 sage leaves
4 thin slices provolone cheese
Salt and freshly ground
    black pepper

1 cup all-purpose flour
4 eggs
½ cup milk
3 cups panko or regular
    fresh breadcrumbs
¼ cup (approx.) canola oil
Grated Parmesan cheese
    for garnish

Give this classic Italian dish a Canadian twist by substituting Oka cheese for the provolone. **SERVES 4**

CARROT-PARSNIP TERRINE In a large saucepan, combine carrots, parsnips, thyme, and bay leaf with enough cold, salted water to cover. Bring to a boil over high heat. Reduce heat to medium-low, then simmer, covered, for 15–20 minutes or until vegetables are very tender. Drain well. While vegetables are still hot, transfer to a food processor. Add butter. Process until a smooth purée forms. Scrape purée into a medium bowl. Let cool to room temperature. Preheat the oven to 350°F.

In a small bowl, whisk together eggs and cream. Whisk egg mixture into vegetable purée, along with salt and pepper to taste. Divide purée among 4 buttered ¾-cup ramekins. Put ramekins in a shallow roasting pan. Pour boiling water into the pan to reach halfway up sides of ramekins. Bake, uncovered, for 35–40 minutes or until terrines are just set. Keep warm.

VEAL Working with 2 cutlets at a time, place the meat between 2 pieces of parchment paper or plastic wrap. Pound with a meat tenderizer or rolling pin until flattened, trying not the rupture the meat.

In a small bowl, stir together mustard and honey. Spread half the mustard mixture over 1 side of each of 4 cutlets. Top each with 1 slice prosciutto, 3 sage leaves, then 1 slice provolone. Spread remaining mustard mixture over 1 side of each of remaining cutlets. Place cutlets over cheese, mustard side down, to make 4 "sandwiches." Sprinkle veal with salt and pepper to taste.

Spread flour in a shallow dish. In a separate shallow dish, whisk together eggs and milk. In a third dish, spread breadcrumbs. Dust veal with flour to coat completely. Dip veal in egg mixture to coat completely. Coat evenly with breadcrumbs, pressing firmly so crumbs adhere.

Preheat the oven to 375°F. In a large heavy skillet, heat 1 Tbsp oil over medium-high heat. Add as many pieces of veal as will fit in a single layer. Cook for 3–5 minutes, turning once, until golden brown on both sides. Remove veal to a large baking sheet as each batch browns. Repeat with remaining veal, adding more oil as necessary. When all veal is browned, transfer baking sheet to oven. Cook for 5–7 minutes or until tender.

TO SERVE Cut each piece of veal in half. Divide among 4 plates. Sprinkle veal with Parmesan cheese. Serve with carrot-parsnip terrine and Black-Olive Gnocchi (see page 77).

Andy "Fireball" Robidoux
SOUS CHEF

THROUGHOUT ONE OF THE RECIPE TESTING sessions, Andy "Fireball" Robiloux regaled us with the sight and the process of his new mullet. A pure-1980s, right-off-the-ice mullet. At the end of the session, as Keith Farkas packed the plastic bins of cookware, Fireball made the off-hand comment, "Just needs a couple of racing stripes right here," stroking his temples.

"I have clippers," replied Christa Moffat.

Minutes later, a towel draped around his shoulders, Fireball sat on a stool out on the deck and received two stripes on one side and three on the other.

"After high school I didn't have a lot of options. Being a chef seemed the best. I went to a one-year culinary arts program at Canadore College.

"Since then I've cooked in every kind of restaurant—big hotels, little hotels, yacht clubs, dives, pubs, you name it.

"At the Lodge we don't have to worry about the budget. We have a lot of freedom to cook what we want without worrying about the money. Creative with no restraint. We do what we want and the guests want."

He laughs and shakes his mullet. "It's all about really, really great food."

"You think of any other questions, let me know." With a wave, he says, "Sweet man, later," and he's off.

Grilled Organic Beef Tenderloin
with Potato Gratin

POTATO GRATIN

½ cup butter

2 large Kennebec or baking
   potatoes, peeled and
   thinly sliced

½ large sweet potato, peeled
   and thinly sliced

1 cup whipping cream

½ onion, finely diced

½ cup finely shredded
   provolone cheese

1 tsp finely chopped
   fresh thyme

½ tsp grated nutmeg

Salt and freshly ground
   black pepper

GARNISH

¼ lb thick-cut bacon, diced

½ onion, finely diced

1 Tbsp butter

12 stalks asparagus, trimmed
   and blanched

Salt and freshly ground
   black pepper

STEAK

4 pieces beef tenderloin
   (each about 6 oz)

3 Tbsp olive oil

Salt

¼ cup ground pink peppercorns

4 pinches fleur de sel

Red wine veal jus (see
   page 123)

There are some nights when only a steak will do. This one is given special-occasion status with a pink peppercorn crust and a rich potato gratin. Begin preparing the potato gratin a day ahead. For best results slice potatoes and sweet potatoes using a mandoline slicer. **SERVES 4**

POTATO GRATIN Preheat the oven to 350°F. Line an 8-inch square baking dish with foil, leaving a 2-inch overhang on 2 sides. Grease foil generously with some of the butter. In a large bowl, combine potatoes, sweet potato, and cream. Meanwhile, in a small skillet, melt 1 Tbsp butter over medium heat. Add onion. Cook, stirring, for 5–7 minutes or until soft and golden brown.

Set aside half of cheese for garnish. Remove potatoes and sweet potatoes from cream, shaking off excess cream (discard any cream remaining in bowl). Arrange half of regular potato in prepared dish, making 3 thin layers and sprinkling each layer with a little onion, cheese, thyme, nutmeg, and salt and pepper to taste. Top with all of the sweet potato, making 4 thin layers, and sprinkling each layer with flavourings as before. Finish with 3 thin layers of regular potato, sprinkling each layer with remaining onion, cheese, thyme, nutmeg, and salt and pepper to taste.

Cover dish with foil. Press down firmly on gratin. Bake, covered, for 1–1½ hours or until potatoes are tender. Let cool to room temperature. Refrigerate, covered, overnight. When ready to serve, preheat the oven to 350°F. Use foil overhang to remove gratin from dish. Trim edges. Cut gratin into 3- × 2-inch portions. Put gratin portions on a baking sheet. Sprinkle tops with remaining cheese. Heat in oven for about 15 minutes or until hot.

continued on page 122 . . .

Grilled Organic Beef Tenderloin with Potato Gratin *(continued)*

GARNISH In a small skillet over medium-high heat, cook bacon and onion, stirring often, for 6–8 minutes or until bacon is crisp and onion is soft but not brown. Keep warm. In a large skillet, melt butter over medium heat. Add asparagus, and salt and pepper to taste. Cook, tossing occasionally, for 3–5 minutes or until asparagus is tender-crisp. Keep warm.

STEAK Let steaks stand at room temperature for 30 minutes before cooking. Rub steaks all over with olive oil. Sprinkle with salt to taste. Spread peppercorns out on a plate. Roll sides of each steak in peppercorns to coat well. Preheat the barbecue to high. Grill steaks for 6–8 minutes, turning once, for medium-rare. Remove steaks to a warm platter. Let rest for 5 minutes before serving.

TO SERVE Reheat red wine veal jus. Place a steak on each of 4 plates. Place asparagus alongside. Sprinkle steaks with fleur de sel. Set a piece of reheated gratin alongside each steak. Drizzle with red wine veal jus. Garnish with bacon mixture.

Grilled Organic T-Bones
with Red Wine Veal Jus

RED WINE VEAL JUS
¾ lb beef trimmings
5 cups veal stock (see page 176)
1⅔ cups red wine
2 stalks celery, coarsely
   chopped
1 medium onion, coarsely
   chopped
1 medium carrot, coarsely
   chopped
1 handful parsley stems
6 cloves garlic, crushed
6 sprigs thyme
1 Tbsp coarsely chopped
   fresh rosemary

Salt and freshly ground black
   pepper

BABY BAKERS
8 baby Yukon gold potatoes,
   scrubbed
2 Tbsp olive oil
Salt
4 thin slices prosciutto

GARNISH
20 grape tomatoes
2 tsp olive oil
Salt and freshly ground
   black pepper

2 Tbsp chicken stock
   (see page 176)
1 Tbsp butter
12 pieces broccolini, trimmed
   and blanched

STEAK
4 organic beef T-bone steaks
   (each about 12 oz)
3 Tbsp olive oil
Salt and freshly ground
   black pepper
4 pinches fleur de sel
½ cup sour cream
1 Tbsp finely chopped chives

With our own beef raised at the bottom of the hill, and long-term relationships with other organic ranchers in the area, the Lodge has the luxury of consistently offering the finest cuts in organic beef. Their taste and tenderness are without equal, as in this simple grilled T-bone. Fleur de sel is grey sea salt from France. Look for veal stock in specialty grocery stores, or make your own (see page 176). **SERVES 4**

RED WINE VEAL JUS Preheat the oven to 400°F. Spread beef trimmings out in a shallow roasting pan. Roast for 20 minutes or until well browned. In a large pot, combine beef trimmings, veal stock, red wine, celery, onion, carrot, parsley stems, garlic, and thyme. Bring to a boil over high heat. Reduce heat to medium-low, then simmer, partially covered, for 4 hours.

Strain through a sieve lined with cheesecloth, discarding solids. Return liquid to the pot. Bring to a boil over high heat, then boil until liquid reduces by half. Stir in rosemary and salt and pepper to taste. Let cool. Refrigerate until ready to serve.

BABY BAKERS Preheat the oven to 375°F. In a shallow roasting pan, toss potatoes, olive oil, and salt to taste. Roast for 25–35 minutes or until tender. Keep warm. Arrange prosciutto on a large baking sheet lined with parchment paper. Bake for 10–12 minutes or until crisp. Break each slice in half. Set aside.

GARNISH In a medium bowl, toss tomatoes with olive oil, and salt and pepper to taste. Spread out on a rimmed baking sheet. Ignite a blowtorch. Play torch over tomatoes, turning often, until lightly charred all over. Alternatively, broil 4 inches from hot broiler for 8–10 minutes, turning often, until lightly charred all over. Meanwhile, in a small skillet,

continued on page 125 . . .

Grilled Organic T-Bones with Red Wine Veal Jus *(continued)*

heat chicken stock and butter over medium heat until butter melts. Add broccolini, and more salt and pepper to taste. Cook, stirring occasionally, just until heated through. Keep warm.

STEAK Let steaks stand at room temperature for 30 minutes before cooking. Rub steaks all over with olive oil. Sprinkle with salt and pepper to taste. Preheat the barbecue to high. Grill steaks for 6–8 minutes, turning once, for medium-rare. Remove steaks to a warm platter. Let rest for 5 minutes before serving.

TO SERVE Reheat red wine veal jus. Spoon some jus on each of 4 plates. Put a steak on each pool of jus. Sprinkle steaks with fleur de sel. Cut each potato almost in half. Put 2 potatoes on each plate. Top potatoes with sour cream, chives, and a piece of prosciutto. Garnish plates with tomatoes and broccolini.

Walnut-Crusted Pork Tenderloin

FENNEL MASH

3 fennel bulbs, trimmed

¼ cup olive oil

Salt and freshly ground
black pepper

4 russet potatoes, peeled
and cut into chunks

½ cup whipping cream

¼ cup butter

Sambuca liqueur to taste

ROSEMARY-FIG JUS

1 cup dried figs, cut in half

1 cup red wine

1 Tbsp butter

1 small shallot, minced

2 cups veal stock (see page 176)

3 sprigs rosemary

Salt and freshly ground
black pepper

Granulated sugar to taste

WALNUT-CRUSTED PORK

1 Tbsp butter

1 onion, finely diced

1 small sweet red pepper,
seeded and finely diced

8 Granny Smith apples, peeled,
cored, and diced

3 Tbsp five-spice powder

2 Tbsp granulated sugar

2 Tbsp cider vinegar

Salt and freshly ground
black pepper

2 pork tenderloins (each
about 12 oz–1 lb), trimmed
of excess fat

1 egg

1 Tbsp milk

4 cups walnut halves,
finely ground

2 cups all-purpose flour

2 Tbsp canola oil

Pork and apples are a marriage made in heaven. Here the fruit forms a tasty stuffing for nut-crusted tenderloins. **SERVES 4**

FENNEL MASH Preheat the oven to 350°F. In a shallow roasting pan, toss fennel bulbs with oil, and salt and pepper to taste. Cover tightly with foil. Roast for about 2 hours or until fennel bulbs become tender and slightly caramelized. Meanwhile, put potatoes in a large saucepan with enough cold, salted water to cover them. Bring to a boil over high heat. Reduce heat to medium-low, then simmer, covered, for 25–30 minutes or until tender. Drain well.

Chop fennel coarsely. Pass fennel and potatoes through a food mill or rub through a fine sieve. Return to the saucepan used to cook potatoes. Stir in cream, butter, and Sambuca, and more salt and pepper to taste. Keep warm.

ROSEMARY-FIG JUS In a medium saucepan, combine figs and wine. Bring to a boil over medium-high heat. Reduce heat to medium-low, then simmer, covered, for about 30 minutes or until figs are tender. Remove figs. Set aside. Boil wine over medium heat until it reduces by half.

In a separate medium saucepan, melt butter over medium heat. Add shallot. Cook, stirring often, for 3–5 minutes or until shallot is soft but not brown. Add reduced wine. Bring to a boil, using a wooden spoon to scrape up any browned bits from bottom of saucepan. Add stock and rosemary. Bring back to a boil over medium-high heat. Reduce heat to medium, then simmer until liquid reduces by half. Discard rosemary. Add figs to sauce. Season with salt, pepper, and sugar to taste. Keep warm.

continued on page 128 . . .

Walnut-Crusted Pork Tenderloin *(continued)*

WALNUT-CRUSTED PORK In a medium saucepan, melt butter over medium heat. Add onion and red pepper. Cook, stirring often, for 3–5 minutes or until soft but not brown. Add apples. Cook, stirring, for 2 minutes. Remove saucepan from the heat. Stir in five-spice powder, sugar, vinegar, and salt and pepper to taste. Let cool completely.

Cut each pork tenderloin lengthwise, cutting almost but not quite through. Open up each tenderloin like a book. Spoon half of apple mixture along length of each tenderloin. Tie tenderloins with butcher's twine to enclose stuffing.

In a small bowl, beat together egg and milk. In a shallow dish, stir together walnuts and flour. Brush tenderloins all over with egg mixture. Roll tenderloins in walnut mixture to coat completely, patting nut coating so that it adheres.

Preheat the oven to 400°F. Heat a large heavy ovenproof skillet over medium-high heat, then add oil. Cook tenderloins, turning often, for 5–7 minutes or until browned on all sides. Transfer skillet to the oven and roast for 18–20 minutes or until a meat thermometer inserted into thickest past of tenderloin registers 145°F. Remove pork to a cutting board. Let rest for 5 minutes before serving.

TO SERVE Cut each tenderloin diagonally into thick slices. Divide pork among 4 plates. Spoon fennel mash alongside each portion. Garnish plates with rosemary-fig jus. Serve with steamed carrots.

Grilled Venison Tenderloin
with Wild Rice Blini

SHALLOT SALSA
6 shallots, peeled
3 Tbsp olive oil
⅓ cup gin
1 Tbsp champagne vinegar
    or good-quality white
    wine vinegar
½ cup cherry or grape tomatoes,
    halved
1 Tbsp minced garlic
Liquid honey to taste
Salt and freshly ground
    black pepper

WILD RICE BLINI
1 cup cooked wild rice
2 cups rice flour
1 tsp baking powder
1 cup milk
2 eggs
1 Tbsp minced garlic
Salt and freshly ground
    black pepper

GRILLED VENISON
TENDERLOIN
4 pieces venison tenderloin
    (each about 4–6 oz)
2 Tbsp olive oil
1 Tbsp ground juniper berries
Salt and freshly ground
    black pepper

For years the Lodge has worked with Hills Meats on the Lower Mainland to source the finest in wild game. Their meat is tender and retains just the right amount of gamey flavour. **SERVES 4**

SHALLOT SALSA Preheat the oven to 350°F. In a small bowl, toss shallots with 1 Tbsp oil until well coated. Wrap loosely in foil. Roast for about 1 hour or until tender. When cool enough to handle, chop shallots finely. Set aside. Meanwhile, in a small saucepan, stir together gin and vinegar. Bring to a boil over medium-high heat. Remove from the heat. Let cool to room temperature.

In a medium serving bowl, stir together gin mixture, shallots, remaining oil, tomatoes, garlic, and honey, and salt and pepper to taste.

WILD RICE BLINI Spread cooked wild rice out on a baking sheet. Let stand at room temperature for about 1 hour or until dry. Sprinkle rice flour and baking powder over rice. In a medium bowl, whisk together milk, eggs, garlic, and salt and pepper to taste. Stir rice mixture into milk mixture just until combined. Heat a good-quality non-stick skillet over medium-high heat. Drop spoonfuls of blini batter into skillet. Cook for 4–6 minutes, turning once, until golden. Repeat with remaining batter. Keep warm until ready to serve.

GRILLED VENISON TENDERLOIN Preheat the barbecue to high. Rub tenderloin pieces with oil. Sprinkle with juniper berries, and salt and pepper to taste. Grill for about 3 minutes on each side for rare to medium-rare.

TO SERVE Place each piece of tenderloin on a blini. Garnish with shallot salsa.

Pan-Roasted Pork with Spiced Mango Coulis

SPICED MANGO COULIS
1 Tbsp canola oil
1 large onion, finely diced
3 very ripe mangoes, peeled, pitted, and diced
2 cups dry white wine
5 whole star anise

VEGETABLES
12–16 baby potatoes, scrubbed
6 shallots, minced
¼ cup olive oil
3 sprigs thyme
1 sprig rosemary
Salt and freshly ground black pepper
1 Tbsp butter
8 baby carrots, blanched
2 Tbsp orange or almond liqueur
1 lemon
12 stalks asparagus, trimmed

PORK
2 pork tenderloins (each about 12 oz–1 lb), trimmed of excess fat
Salt and freshly ground black pepper
2 Tbsp olive oil
1 lime
Whole star anise for garnish
Finely chopped chives for garnish

Pairing mango with pork tenderloin adds a touch of the exotic to a simple dish. For the prettiest plate, choose multicoloured organic baby carrots. **SERVES 4**

SPICED MANGO COULIS In a medium saucepan, heat oil over medium heat. Add onion, cook, stirring often, for 5–7 minutes or until onion is soft but not brown. Add mangoes, white wine, and star anise. Bring to a boil over medium-high heat. Reduce heat to medium-low, then simmer, uncovered, until almost all of wine has evaporated. Remove saucepan from the heat. Let cool slightly. In a food processor, process mango mixture until almost smooth. Rub through a fine sieve into a heatproof bowl. Set aside.

VEGETABLES Preheat the oven to 375°F. In a shallow roasting pan, toss potatoes with shallots, 2 Tbsp of the oil, thyme, rosemary, and salt and pepper to taste. Roast, uncovered, for 30–40 minutes, stirring occasionally, until crisp on the outside and tender inside. Set aside and keep warm.

In a small skillet over medium heat, melt butter. Add carrots and liqueur. Cook, stirring often, for 8–10 minutes or until carrots are tender-crisp. Keep warm.

Preheat the barbecue to high. Squeeze juice from lemon into a medium bowl. Add aspara-gus, remaining 2 Tbsp olive oil, and more salt and pepper to taste. Toss together well. Grill asparagus, turning often, for 3–5 minutes or until tender-crisp. Keep warm.

PORK Preheat the oven to 400°F. Sprinkle pork tenderloins with salt and pepper to taste. Heat a large heavy ovenproof skillet over medium-high heat, then add oil. Cook tenderloins, turning often, for 8–10 minutes or until browned on all sides. Transfer skillet to the oven. Roast for 15–18 minutes or until a meat thermometer inserted into thickest part of tenderloin registers 145°F. Remove pork to a cutting board. Let rest for 5 minutes before serving.

TO SERVE Set bowl of spiced mango coulis over a saucepan of simmering water to reheat. Squeeze lime juice into coulis, then stir well. Cut each tenderloin diagonally into 6 thick slices. Divide potatoes, carrots, and asparagus evenly among 4 plates. Stack 3 slices of pork next to each portion of vegetables. Spoon spiced mango coulis onto each plate. Garnish with star anise and chives.

Poached Rack of Lamb with Mint Gastrique

MINT GASTRIQUE

3 cups champagne vinegar or
  good-quality white wine
  vinegar
2 cups granulated sugar
1 cup finely chopped fresh mint
Grated zest of 1 lemon
Salt and freshly ground
  black pepper

LAMB

2 large lamb racks
  (each about 1 lb)
9 cups olive oil
8 cloves garlic, peeled
2 medium shallots, coarsely
  chopped
5 sprigs rosemary
4 sprigs thyme

2 bay leaves
Salt and freshly ground
  black pepper

This unusual way of cooking lamb—poached in olive oil—renders the meat sweet and juicy. The kitchen at the Lodge uses Portuguese olive oil, but any good-quality fruity variety will do. A minty sweet and tart reduction, called a gastrique, *adds the finishing touch. Serve with Baby Bakers (see page 123).* SERVES 4

MINT GASTRIQUE In a medium non-reactive saucepan, stir together vinegar and sugar. Bring to a boil over high heat. Boil until liquid reduces and becomes syrupy. Remove from the heat. Let cool slightly. Stir in mint, lemon zest, and salt and pepper to taste. Set aside until ready to serve.

LAMB Trim lamb racks of any excess fat and silver skin. If racks haven't been "Frenched," scrape meat and fat away from ends of bones. Set a large heatproof bowl over a large pot of simmering water. Pour oil into bowl. Add garlic, shallots, rosemary, thyme, and bay leaves. Heat oil until a meat thermometer registers 130°F.

Sprinkle lamb racks generously with salt and pepper. Immerse lamb racks in oil (it's okay if ends of the bones aren't submerged). Poach the lamb for a minimum of 25 minutes, or up to 2 hours, ensuring the oil stays between 130°F and 135°F. Check temperature often—as long as the oil stays below 135°F, the meat will not overcook.

Just before serving, heat a large heavy skillet over high heat. Remove lamb racks from oil. Cook lamb racks in skillet for 5–7 minutes until browned on all sides. Remove lamb to a cutting board. Let rest for 5 minutes before serving.

TO SERVE Cut lamb racks between bones into individual chops. Divide among 4 plates. Drizzle with mint gastrique. Serve with baby bakers (see page 123).

Desserts

White Chocolate and Passion Fruit Mousse

8 oz good-quality white
    chocolate
5 eggs

3 Tbsp granulated sugar
2 cups whipping cream
1 Tbsp unflavoured powdered
    gelatin

¼ cup water
¾ cup passion fruit concentrate
Gooseberries for garnish (or
    other fresh seasonal berries)

This mousse combines two wonderful flavours in each bite. Look for passion fruit concentrate in specialty food stores, or substitute mango concentrate. **SERVES 4–6**

In a heatproof bowl set over a saucepan of simmering water, melt chocolate until almost smooth. Remove bowl from the heat (leave saucepan over heat). Stir chocolate until smooth. Set aside.

In a second heatproof bowl, combine eggs and sugar. Set bowl over saucepan of simmering water. Whisk until egg mixture is thickened, light, and fluffy.

In a medium bowl, whip cream until it holds soft peaks. Set aside. In a separate medium bowl, sprinkle gelatin over water. Set aside for 5 minutes or until puffy.

Meanwhile, in a small saucepan, bring passion fruit concentrate to a boil over medium-high heat. Whisk passion fruit concentrate into gelatin until gelatin is completely dissolved. Gradually whisk passion fruit mixture into egg mixture. Whisk in melted chocolate until well combined. Let cool slightly. Fold whipped cream into passion fruit mixture until no white streaks remain. Spoon into a serving dish. Refrigerate, covered, for at least 3 hours or until set. Garnish each with gooseberries.

NOTE Our pastry chef, Johanne, has dressed this dessert up by adding a chocolate cage (see process photos, right).

Lemon Meringue Tarts with Pumpkin Seed Pastry

PUMPKIN-SEED PASTRY
½ cup unsalted pumpkin seeds
¾ cup all-purpose flour
2 Tbsp granulated sugar
½ cup butter
1 egg yolk

LEMON CURD
1⅓ cups granulated sugar
3 eggs
4 egg yolks (reserve whites
   for meringue)
¾ cup fresh lemon juice
   (from 5 to 8 lemons)
1 cup cold butter, cubed

MERINGUE
4 egg whites
½ cup granulated sugar

Pumpkin seeds add a nutty crispness to the pastry of these delicate lemony tarts. **SERVES 6**

PUMPKIN-SEED PASTRY Preheat the oven to 400°F. Spread pumpkin seeds out on a rimmed baking sheet. Roast for 6–8 minutes, stirring occasionally, until puffed and fragrant. Let cool completely.

In a food processor, process pumpkin seeds until finely ground. Add flour and sugar. Continue to process until well combined. Add butter. Process until mixture resembles coarse crumbs. Add egg yolk and process until dough holds together. Tip dough out onto a sheet of plastic wrap. Form into a ball. Wrap in plastic wrap. Refrigerate for 1 hour. Remove the dough from the refrigerator and let stand at room temperature for 30 minutes before rolling it out.

Preheat the oven to 350°F. On a lightly floured surface, roll out dough to ⅛ inch thickness. (If dough is hard to roll, roll between 2 layers of parchment paper.) Using an 8-inch cookie cutter, cut out circles to line six 5-inch tart shells or large muffin pans. Bake for 8–10 minutes or until golden brown. If pastry puffs up, prick with fork to deflate.

LEMON CURD In a heatproof bowl set over a saucepan of simmering water, whisk sugar, eggs, and egg yolks until well combined. Add lemon juice. Cook, whisking constantly, until mixture is thickened and smooth. Remove bowl from the heat. Whisk in butter until melted. Set bowl in a larger bowl of ice until mixture is cool, stirring occasionally.

MERINGUE Set a heatproof bowl over a saucepan of simmering water. Using an electric mixer, beat egg whites and sugar until a candy thermometer registers 140°F. Remove bowl from the heat. Continue to beat at high speed until meringue is light, fluffy, shiny, and holds stiff peaks.

TO SERVE Fill baked tart shells with lemon curd. Spoon meringue over lemon curd, covering it completely. Using a blowtorch, brown tips of meringue. Serve at once.

Pear Tarte Tatin

¾ cup butter
¾ cup granulated sugar

8 pears, peeled, cored, and
quartered

Half 397-gram package frozen
puff pastry, thawed

This French dessert is traditionally made with apples, but at the Lodge it's become a favourite with local B.C. pears—especially when it's topped with a scoop of ice cream. A cast-iron skillet works best for this. SERVES 8

In a 10-inch cast-iron skillet, melt butter over medium heat. Stir in sugar. Arrange pears decoratively in skillet. Cook, uncovered, for 30–40 minutes or until pears are tender and juices form a caramel sauce. Shake the skillet occasionally to make sure pears aren't sticking or burning to the skillet.

Meanwhile, preheat the oven to 400°F. On a lightly floured surface, roll out pastry to form a 10-inch circle. Remove skillet from the heat and let cool slightly. Lay pastry on top of pears. Transfer skillet to the oven. Bake for 20–25 minutes or until pastry is golden brown.

Let tarte cool slightly. Loosen edges of pastry. Invert a large serving plate over skillet. Invert skillet and plate together, shaking gently to release pears. Serve warm with vanilla ice cream.

Alsatian Apple Pie

PIE CRUST
1 cup all-purpose flour
1 cup whole wheat or spelt flour
Pinch salt
⅔ cup cold butter, cubed
⅓ cup water
1 egg yolk

FILLING
5–6 Granny Smith or Fuji
  apples, peeled, cored, and
  thinly sliced
¼ cup granulated sugar

Pinch cinnamon, or to taste
2 cups whipping cream
1 egg

Apples and pears grow in abundance in Alain's (see page 88) home region of Alsace in eastern France, so his mom would often bake this pie for the family. Serve with your favourite vanilla ice cream. **SERVES 8**

PIE CRUST In a medium bowl, whisk together all-purpose flour, whole wheat flour, and salt. Rub in butter with your fingertips until mixture resembles coarse crumbs. In a small bowl, whisk together water and egg yolk. Make a well in centre of flour mixture. Pour in egg mixture. Blend flour with egg mixture just until dough forms a ball. Wrap in plastic wrap. Refrigerate for 1 hour.

Preheat the oven to 350°F. On a lightly floured surface, roll out dough to ⅛ inch thickness. Fit pastry into a 12-inch pie plate.

FILLING Arrange apples in pie crust in overlapping circles. Sprinkle with 1 Tbsp sugar and cinnamon. Bake for 25 minutes or until apples are almost tender.

Meanwhile, in a medium bowl, whisk together remaining sugar, cream, and egg just until combined. Pour cream mixture over apples. Return pie to oven. Bake for a further 10–15 minutes or until custard sets and turns golden. Let cool to room temperature before serving.

Devil's Food Cake with Raspberry Coulis

CAKE

2⅓ cups granulated sugar
1 ¾ cups all-purpose flour
1 cup unsweetened cocoa
    powder
1 tsp baking powder
1 tsp baking soda
½ tsp salt
1 cup milk
3 eggs

½ cup canola oil
1 Tbsp vanilla
1 ½ cups boiling water

RASPBERRY COULIS

2 cups fresh or frozen
    unsweetened raspberries
2 Tbsp granulated sugar,
    or to taste

BUTTERCREAM

1 egg
1 egg yolk
½ cup granulated sugar
3 Tbsp water
1 cup butter, softened

GANACHE

1 lb good-quality semi-sweet
    or bittersweet chocolate
2 cups whipping cream

Wickedly delicious, this cake is made in four easy steps. **MAKES ONE 9-INCH CAKE**

CAKE Preheat the oven to 350°F. Grease a 9-inch round springform baking pan. Line base with a circle of parchment paper. In a medium bowl, whisk together sugar, flour, cocoa, baking powder, baking soda, and salt. In a separate medium bowl, beat together milk, eggs, oil, and vanilla until well combined. Stir milk mixture into flour mixture until well combined. Stir in boiling water.

Rub batter through a fine sieve set over prepared pan to remove any lumps. Bake for 50–60 minutes or until a toothpick inserted in centre of cake comes out clean. Let cake cool in pan on wire rack for 5 minutes. Release sides of pan. Remove cake from pan. Let cool completely on wire rack. Peel off paper.

RASPBERRY COULIS If using fresh raspberries, reserve a few to decorate the top of cake. In a small saucepan, combine remaining raspberries and sugar. Bring to a boil over medium-high heat. Reduce heat to medium-low, then simmer for 5 minutes or until raspberries soften. Rub through a fine sieve to remove seeds. Taste coulis and add more sugar if necessary (cake will be rich so coulis should remain slightly tart). Set aside.

BUTTERCREAM In a medium bowl, beat egg and egg yolk until pale. In a small saucepan,

stir together sugar and water. Bring to a boil over medium-high heat, stirring to dissolve sugar. Boil until a candy thermometer registers 235°F, or a little of the syrup dropped into ice water forms a soft ball. Beating constantly, slowly add syrup to eggs. Continue to beat until mixture is cool. Gradually whisk in butter until well combined.

Split cooled cake in half horizontally. Spread half of raspberry coulis over bottom layer. Replace top of cake. Spread remaining coulis over top of cake. Spread buttercream over top and sides of cake to cover it completely. Set cake on a rack over a baking sheet lined with parchment paper. Refrigerate for about 45 minutes or until buttercream sets.

GANACHE In a medium heatproof bowl set over a saucepan of simmering water, melt chocolate until almost smooth. Remove bowl from the heat. Stir chocolate until smooth. In a medium saucepan, bring cream to a boil over medium-high heat. Whisk cream into chocolate until well combined. Let cool slightly until warm but still liquid.

Carefully pour ganache over buttercream-frosted cake to cover it completely. (Reheat any fallen ganache and serve over ice cream.) Refrigerate cake for 1 hour or until ganache sets. Garnish with reserved raspberries.

White Chocolate and Raspberry Crème Brûlée

½ cup fresh raspberries
7 oz good-quality white
chocolate

6 egg yolks
⅓ cup granulated sugar

2 cups whipping cream
⅓ cup packed brown sugar

Here's everyone's favourite dessert, dressed up in its very best—white chocolate and raspberries.
SERVES 4

Preheat the oven to 300°F. Divide raspberries among four ¾-cup ramekins. In a medium heatproof bowl set over a saucepan of simmering water, melt chocolate until almost smooth. Remove bowl from the heat. Stir chocolate until smooth. Set aside.

In a medium bowl, whisk together egg yolks and granulated sugar until well combined. In a medium saucepan, bring cream to a boil over medium-high heat. Whisking constantly, gradually pour cream into egg yolk mixture. Strain cream mixture through a fine sieve into bowl containing chocolate. Whisk until smooth.

Pour cream mixture into ramekins, dividing evenly. Put ramekins in a shallow roasting pan. Pour boiling water into pan to reach halfway up sides of ramekins. Bake, uncovered, for 50–60 minutes or until custards are set but centres still jiggle slightly. Let cool slightly. Refrigerate for at least 3 hours or overnight.

Before serving, sprinkle brown sugar evenly over top of each custard. With a blowtorch, caramelize the sugar, moving blowtorch constantly to ensure sugar doesn't burn. Serve at once.

Kerri Maier
PASTRY AND MORNING CHEF

WHEN ASKED ABOUT HOW SHE BECAME A chef, she laughs, "It always starts with grandmas. Walking into her house. The smells. Always baking apple pies, baking bread," she pauses. "She had a passion for baking and it rubbed off on me. I hope it rubs off on my daughters, too."

Kerri graduated from University of Saskatchewan with a degree in archeology and after working a couple years in her field, tossed it to move to Fernie.

"My sister lived in Fernie and I always visited on university breaks and vacations. I came for the town, not the skiing. I loved it here. Then I learned to ski."

About being a chef at Island Lake Lodge, she says, "It's the best job in the world. Every day is different. Showing up at 5:30 in the morning and getting on a sled to go to work. Even sometimes being chased by a moose. The physical surroundings do something to you. It gets to you. The scenery and the adventure."

KERRI'S RECIPES
- Tangy Lemon Squares (page 158)
- Toffee Almond Squares (page 161)
- Raspberry Streusel Squares (page 162)
- Decadent Brownie Cookies (page 165)
- Oatmeal Jam Cookies (page 166)
- Rich Shortbread Fingers (page 168)
- Sour Cream Raspberry Loaf (page 169)
- Chocolate Mocha Loaf (page 172)

Tiramisu

LADYFINGER COOKIES

6 eggs, separated
1 cup granulated sugar
1 tsp fresh lemon juice
¾ cup cornstarch
1 cup all-purpose flour

MASCARPONE MOUSSE

2 cups mascarpone (Italian cream cheese)
2 cups whipping cream
¾ cup icing sugar
6 egg yolks
1½ Tbsp unflavoured powdered gelatin

¼ cup water
½ cup coffee liqueur, such as Tia Maria or Kahlúa
2 cups cold black coffee
¼ cup unsweetened cocoa powder

Johanne (see page 8) makes her own ladyfinger cookies for the Lodge's tiramisu; no wonder it tastes so good! **SERVES 8–10**

LADYFINGER COOKIES Preheat the oven to 400°F. Line a large baking sheet with parchment paper. In a medium bowl and using an electric mixer, beat egg yolks and ⅓ cup sugar until thickened and pale. In a large bowl and using an electric mixer with clean beaters, beat egg whites, ⅓ cup sugar, and the lemon juice until egg whites triple in volume and hold soft peaks. In a small bowl, stir together cornstarch and remaining sugar. Gradually beat cornstarch mixture into egg whites until mixture holds stiff peaks. Gradually fold egg yolk mixture into whites until well combined. Fold in flour.

Spoon batter into a piping bag fitted with a plain nozzle. Pipe batter into 3- or 4-inch rounds on prepared baking sheet. Alternatively, spoon batter into rounds on baking sheet and flatten with the back of a spoon. Bake for about 8 minutes or until cookies are browned and dry. Let cookies cool on baking sheet for 5 minutes. Remove cookies with a spatula. Let cool completely on wire racks.

MASCARPONE MOUSSE In a medium heat-proof bowl set over a saucepan of simmering water, heat mascarpone just until softened. Remove from the heat. In a separate medium bowl, whip cream until it holds soft peaks. In a large bowl, beat icing sugar and egg yolks until thick and pale.

In a small bowl, sprinkle gelatin over water. Set aside for 5 minutes or until puffy. In a small saucepan, bring liqueur to a boil over medium-high heat. Whisk liqueur into gelatin. Return liqueur mixture to saucepan. Whisk over low heat until gelatin is completely dissolved. Whisk liqueur mixture into egg yolk mixture until well combined. Fold in mascarpone. Let cool slightly. Fold in whipped cream until well combined. Refrigerate, covered, for 3 hours or until set.

TO ASSEMBLE Dip 1 of the bigger cookies in coffee, then place it on a cookie sheet. Spoon some mousse onto cookie. Sprinkle lightly with cocoa. Repeat layers, using 3 more cookies and ending with a cookie as the top layer (use smaller cookies for tops of desserts). Repeat with remaining cookies, cocoa, and mousse to make 8–10 towers in all. Serve at once.

Chocolate Fruit Flan

SWEET DOUGH CRUST
¾ cup butter, softened
¼ cup granulated sugar
1 egg
1 tsp vanilla
Pinch salt
1 cup all-purpose flour
Icing sugar for rolling pastry

FILLING
4 oz good-quality semi-sweet or
   bittersweet chocolate
¾ cup granulated sugar
4 eggs
2 cups whipping cream
1 tsp vanilla

Fresh seasonal fruit such as
   raspberries, blueberries,
   strawberries, kiwi fruit, etc.
3 oz chocolate, melted (optional)

This flan offers a surprise inside, and is the perfect, light finish to any day on the slopes. **SERVES 6**

SWEET DOUGH CRUST In a medium bowl, beat together butter and sugar until pale and fluffy. Beat in egg until well combined. Beat in vanilla and salt. Beat in flour until well combined. Gather dough into a ball. Wrap in plastic wrap. Refrigerate for at least 2 hours, preferably overnight.

One hour before preparing tart, remove pastry from fridge. Dust work surface with icing sugar. Roll out pastry to form a 12-inch circle. Fit pastry into a lightly greased 10-inch tart pan. Trim off excess pastry. Refrigerate while you make the filling.

FILLING Preheat the oven to 350°F. In a medium heatproof bowl set over a saucepan of simmering water, melt chocolate until almost smooth. Remove bowl from the heat. Stir chocolate until smooth. In a separate medium bowl, whisk together sugar and eggs until well combined. Whisk in cream and vanilla.

With a pastry brush, paint chocolate all over inside of pastry crust. Strain egg mixture through a fine sieve into tart shell. Bake for 35–40 minutes or until custard is set but centre still jiggles slightly. Let cool completely on a wire rack.

Just before serving, top custard with fresh seasonal fruit. Garnish with whipped cream and drizzle with chocolate, if desired.

Champagne Sabayon and Berry Parfait

SABAYON
¾ cup granulated sugar
½ cup brut champagne or other
   dry white sparkling wine

2 eggs
2 egg yolks
6 Tbsp cold butter, cubed

TO FINISH
6 cups fresh berries
Whipped cream for garnish

This special dessert, usually served on the Lodge's barbecue-themed nights, attracts locals like bees to honey, and creates a fine finish to a dinner of grilled meats. Use whatever berries are in season.
SERVES 6

SABAYON In a large heatproof bowl set over a saucepan of simmering water, whisk together sugar, champagne, eggs, and egg yolks. Whisking constantly, cook for about 15 minutes or until whisk leaves a trail and mixture thickens. Remove bowl from the heat. Whisk in butter 1 piece at a time, allowing each piece to melt before adding more. Refrigerate sabayon, covered, for at least 2 hours or until cool.

TO SERVE In 6 parfait dishes or glasses, layer berries and sabayon, starting with berries and ending with sabayon. Garnish with whipped cream.

Funnel Cakes with Ice Cream and Berry Compote

❧

BERRY COMPOTE
4–6 cups fresh berries
¼ cup granulated sugar
¼ cup finely chopped fresh mint

BATTER
2 cups milk
3 eggs
3 cups all-purpose flour
¼ cup granulated sugar
2 Tbsp baking powder

½ tsp salt
Canola oil for deep-frying
Icing sugar for dusting
Ice cream to serve
Mint sprigs for garnish

These crispy, fried funnel cakes are a decadent way to end any meal. For the topping, add your favourite ice cream and a selection of seasonal berries. **SERVES 6–8**

BERRY COMPOTE In a medium saucepan, stir together berries and sugar. Cook over medium heat for 5–10 minutes or until thick and syrupy but berries are not broken up. Remove from the heat. Stir in mint. Let cool completely.

BATTER In a medium bowl, whisk together milk and eggs until well combined. In a large bowl, whisk together flour, sugar, baking powder, and salt. Whisk milk mixture into flour mixture until a smooth batter forms.

In a deep-fat fryer and following manufacturer's instructions, heat oil to 350°F. Alternatively, half-fill a large pot with oil. Heat over medium-high heat until a candy thermometer registers 350°F. If using a pot, adjust heat as necessary to maintain correct temperature. Have a baking sheet lined with paper towel ready.

Transfer batter into a pitcher with a fine spout. Pour about ¾ cup batter into hot oil, starting in centre of pot and working your way out in a circular motion. Fry for 5–7 minutes, turning once, until golden brown on both sides. Remove cake with a slotted spoon and transfer to the prepared baking sheet. Dust with icing sugar. Repeat with remaining batter to make 6–8 cakes.

TO SERVE Place each funnel cake on a plate and scoop berry compote into centre. Top with ice cream and garnish with mint sprigs.

Squares & Cookies

Tangy Lemon Squares

BASE
¾ cup butter, softened
½ cup granulated sugar
2 cups all-purpose flour
¼ tsp salt

TOPPING
1½ cups granulated sugar
4 eggs
¼ cup all-purpose flour

⅓ cup fresh lemon juice
2 Tbsp grated lemon zest

Kerri (see page 146) claims to have been kissed by grateful strangers who've fallen in love with these luscious lemon squares. They're the all-time favourite of both guests and staff. **MAKES ABOUT 24 SQUARES**

BASE Preheat the oven to 325°F. Grease a 13- × 9-inch baking pan. In a medium bowl, beat butter and sugar until fluffy and pale. Stir in flour and salt just until dough is crumbly. Pat dough evenly over base of prepared pan. Bake for about 30 minutes or until golden brown.

TOPPING In a medium bowl, beat together sugar and eggs until well combined. Beat in flour, lemon juice, and lemon zest. Pour topping over crust. Return pan to oven and bake for a further 20 minutes or until topping sets. Let cool completely in pan on wire rack. Cut into squares.

Toffee Almond Squares

BASE
1 ½ cups all-purpose flour
2 tsp baking powder
2 cups packed brown sugar
2 eggs
½ cup melted butter
1½ tsp vanilla

TOPPING
⅓ cup granulated sugar
⅓ cup corn syrup
¼ cup butter
1 Tbsp water
Pinch salt

1½ cups sliced almonds
2 oz good-quality semi-sweet or
   bittersweet chocolate

You'll find that these squares aren't too sweet, but just sweet enough. They look very impressive drizzled with dark chocolate. **MAKES ABOUT 24 SQUARES**

BASE Preheat the oven to 350°F. Line a 13- × 9-inch baking pan with parchment paper. In a small bowl, whisk together flour and baking powder. In a medium bowl, beat together sugar and eggs until well combined. Beat in butter and vanilla. Fold in flour mixture until well combined. Scrape batter into prepared pan. Bake for about 20 minutes or until a toothpick inserted into centre of base comes out clean.

TOPPING In a small saucepan, heat sugar, syrup, butter, water, and salt over medium heat, stirring until melted. Bring to a boil, then boil gently for 4 minutes. Pour over base. Sprinkle evenly with almonds. Return pan to the oven and bake for a further 15 minutes or until just set. Let cool completely in pan on wire rack.

In a small heatproof bowl set over a saucepan of simmering water, melt chocolate until almost smooth. Remove bowl from the heat. Stir chocolate until smooth. With the tines of a fork, drizzle chocolate evenly over almonds. Set aside until chocolate sets. Cut into squares.

Raspberry Streusel Squares

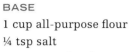

BASE

1 cup all-purpose flour

¼ tsp salt

1 cup granulated sugar

½ cup butter, softened

2 eggs

3 Tbsp fresh orange juice

1 ½ tsp grated orange zest

1 ½ cups fresh raspberries

STREUSEL TOPPING

¼ cup all-purpose flour

¼ cup granulated sugar

1 tsp grated orange zest

1 ½ Tbsp cold butter

This moist and fruity square, with a citrus-spiked streusel topping, is another favourite with skiers at the Lodge. **MAKES ABOUT 24 SQUARES**

BASE Preheat the oven to 300°F. Line a 13- × 9-inch baking pan with parchment paper. In a small bowl, whisk together flour and salt. In a medium bowl, beat together sugar and butter until pale and fluffy. Beat in eggs, orange juice, and orange zest. Fold in flour mixture until well combined. Scrape batter into prepared pan. Scatter evenly with raspberries.

STREUSEL TOPPING In a small bowl, whisk together flour, sugar, and orange zest. Cut in butter until mixture resembles coarse crumbs. Sprinkle topping evenly over raspberries. Bake for 25–30 minutes or until golden brown. Let cool completely in pan on wire rack. Cut into squares.

Decadent Brownie Cookies

4 oz good-quality semi-sweet chocolate
⅓ cup butter
2 oz good-quality unsweetened chocolate

½ cup all-purpose flour
1½ tsp instant coffee granules
¼ tsp baking powder
¼ tsp salt
¾ cup granulated sugar

2 eggs
¾ cup semi-sweet chocolate chips
12 whole pecans for garnish

With their crackled and shiny tops, these cookies resemble brownies and taste just as good. Chocoholics are magnetically drawn to them! **MAKES 12 COOKIES**

In a small heatproof bowl set over a saucepan of simmering water, melt semi-sweet chocolate, butter, and unsweetened chocolate until almost smooth. Remove bowl from the heat. Stir until smooth. Set aside to cool.

In a small bowl, whisk together flour, coffee granules, baking powder, and salt. In a medium bowl, beat together sugar and eggs until well combined. Beat chocolate mixture into sugar mixture. Stir in flour mixture until well combined. Stir in chocolate chips. Refrigerate batter, covered, for 1 hour.

Preheat the oven to 350°F. Line a large baking sheet with parchment paper. Drop rounded tablespoonfuls of batter 2 inches apart onto prepared baking sheet. Top each cookie with a pecan. Bake for about 11 minutes or until tops looks dry. Do not overbake. Let cookies cool on baking sheet for 5 minutes. Remove cookies with a spatula. Let cool completely on wire racks.

Oatmeal Jam Cookies

1 cup all-purpose flour
½ tsp baking powder
½ tsp baking soda
½ tsp salt
½ cup granulated sugar

,113.4,

½ cup packed brown sugar
½ butter, softened
1 egg
½ tsp vanilla
1 cup rolled oats

¼ cup jam
2 oz good-quality white
    chocolate (optional)

Oatmeal's not just for breakfast any more. Drizzle these cookies with white chocolate to give them a fancier look. Use your favourite jam. **MAKES ABOUT 24 COOKIES**

Preheat the oven to 350°F. Line a large baking sheet with parchment paper. In a small bowl, whisk together flour, baking powder, baking soda, and salt. In a medium bowl, beat together granulated sugar, brown sugar, and butter until fluffy. Beat in egg and vanilla. Beat in flour mixture until well combined. Stir in oats. If dough is a bit too wet, add a little more flour, or refrigerate dough for 30 minutes.

Form dough into 1-inch balls. Arrange 2 inches apart on prepared baking sheet. Make an indentation in top of each ball, then fill each indentation with jam. Bake for 9–13 minutes or until golden brown. Let cookies cool on baking sheet for 5 minutes. Remove cookies with a spatula. Let cool completely on wire racks.

In a small heatproof bowl set over a saucepan of simmering water, melt chocolate until almost smooth. Remove bowl from the heat. Stir chocolate until smooth. With the tines of a fork, drizzle chocolate evenly over cookies. Set aside until chocolate sets.

Rich Shortbread Fingers

2 cups all-purpose flour
¼ tsp salt
1 cup butter, softened

½ cup icing sugar
1½ tsp vanilla
1 cup ground pecans
    or almonds

Additional icing sugar
    for coating

At Christmas, Kerri's grandma (see page 146) would bake these melt-in-the-mouth shortbread treats, a.k.a. Mexican wedding cakes. At the Lodge, they're served year round because serving them just once a year is not enough for something so special. **MAKES ABOUT 24 FINGERS**

Preheat the oven to 325°F. Grease a large baking sheet. In a small bowl, whisk together flour and salt. In a medium bowl, beat together butter, sugar, and vanilla until pale and fluffy. Beat in flour mixture and nuts until well combined.

Turn dough out onto a lightly floured surface, then divide in half. Form each half into a sausage shape, about 1½ inches thick. Cut each sausage into 2-inch pieces. Arrange cookies 2 inches apart on prepared baking sheet. Bake for about 15 minutes or until just golden and set.

Let cookies cool on baking sheet for 5 minutes. Remove cookies with a spatula. Roll in icing sugar to coat completely. Let cool completely on wire racks.

Sour Cream Raspberry Loaf

1½ cups all-purpose flour
1 tsp baking powder
¼ tsp baking soda
Pinch salt
¾ cup granulated sugar

¼ cup butter, softened
⅓ cup seedless raspberry jam
1 egg
1 egg white
2 tsp grated lemon zest

1 tsp vanilla
¾ cup sour cream
¼ cup sliced almonds

This beautiful loaf sports a crunchy almond topping. **MAKES ONE 8-INCH LOAF**

Preheat the oven to 350°F. Line base and 2 sides of an 8- × 4-inch loaf pan with parchment paper. In a small bowl, whisk together flour, baking powder, baking soda, and salt. In a medium bowl, beat together sugar and butter until pale and fluffy. Beat in jam, egg, egg white, lemon zest, and vanilla. Fold in flour mixture alternately with sour cream, making 3 additions of flour and 2 of sour cream, starting and ending with flour.

Scrape batter into prepared pan. Sprinkle top evenly with almonds. Bake for about 55 minutes or until a toothpick inserted in centre of loaf comes out clean. Let cool in pan on wire rack for 5 minutes. Turn out and let cool completely on wire rack before slicing.

Chocolate Mocha Loaf

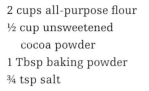

2 cups all-purpose flour
½ cup unsweetened
   cocoa powder
1 Tbsp baking powder
¾ tsp salt

1 cup granulated sugar
¼ cup butter, softened
2 eggs
1 cup milk
1 Tbsp instant coffee granules

1 tsp vanilla
¼ cup semi-sweet chocolate
   chips

This moist loaf is a taste treat for coffee lovers and chocoholics alike. For an extra chocolate kick, add a handful of chocolate chips to the batter. **MAKES ONE 9-INCH LOAF**

Preheat the oven to 350°F. Line base and 2 sides of a 9- × 5-inch loaf pan with parchment paper. In a medium bowl, whisk together flour, cocoa powder, baking powder, and salt. In a separate medium bowl, beat together sugar and butter until pale and fluffy. Beat in eggs 1 at a time. Beat in milk, coffee granules, and vanilla. Fold in flour mixture until well combined.

Scrape batter into prepared pan, then sprinkle top evenly with chocolate chips. Bake for about 1 hour or until a toothpick inserted into centre of loaf comes out clean. Let cool in pan on wire rack for 5 minutes. Turn out and let cool completely on wire rack before slicing.

Basic Recipes

Chicken Stock

MAKES ABOUT 16 CUPS

16 cups water
4 lb chicken bones (no skin)
1 large onion, coarsely chopped
1 large carrot, coarsely chopped
1 large stalk celery, coarsely chopped
1 large leek (white part only), coarsely chopped
3 cloves garlic, peeled
1 tsp black peppercorns
3 sprigs thyme
3 sprigs parsley
2 bay leaves
1 sprig rosemary

In a large stock pot, combine water and chicken bones, making sure water covers bones by at least 3 inches. Bring to a gentle simmer over medium heat, skimming off any scum as it rises to the surface. Continue to skim as stock simmers until no more scum rises.

Add onion, carrot, celery, leek, garlic, peppercorns, thyme, parsley, bay leaves, and rosemary. Bring back to a simmer, then simmer gently, partially covered, for 1 hour. Strain through a colander. Refrigerate for several hours or overnight. Skim off any fat from surface of the stock. Refrigerate stock for up to 3 days, or freeze for up to 3 months.

Veal or Beef Stock

MAKES ABOUT 12 CUPS

5 lb veal or beef bones
1 large onion, coarsely chopped
1 large carrot, coarsely chopped
1 large stalk celery, coarsely chopped
1 Tbsp canola oil
⅓ cup tomato paste
16 cups water
1 small apple, halved
6 cloves garlic, peeled
6 sprigs parsley
6 sprigs thyme
1 Tbsp black peppercorns
3 bay leaves

Preheat the oven to 450°F. Spread bones out in a large shallow roasting pan. Roast for about 2 hours or until browned. In a large bowl, toss together onion, carrot, celery, and oil. Add vegetables to roasting pan. Roast for 20–30 minutes or until bones and vegetables are well browned. Spread tomato paste evenly over vegetables. Roast for a further 15 minutes or until paste is cooked and lightly browned.

Remove bones from roasting pan. In a large stock pot, combine water and bones, making sure water covers bones by at least 3 inches (if not, add more water). Bring to a gentle simmer over medium heat, skimming off any scum as it rises to the surface. Continue to skim as stock simmers until no more scum rises.

Add roasted vegetables to pot, along with apple, garlic, parsley, thyme, peppercorns, and bay leaves. Bring back to a simmer, then simmer gently, partially covered, for 24 hours. Strain through a colander. Refrigerate for several hours or overnight. Skim off any fat from surface of stock. Refrigerate stock for up to 3 days, or freeze for up to 3 months.

Vegetable Stock

MAKES ABOUT 16 CUPS

16 cups water
4 tomatoes, coarsely chopped
1 large onion, coarsely chopped
1 large carrot, coarsely chopped
1 large stalk celery, coarsely chopped
1 large leek (white part only), coarsely chopped
6 cloves garlic, peeled
4 tsp black peppercorns
4 bay leaves
4 sprigs parsley
4 sprigs thyme

In a large stock pot, combine water, tomatoes, onion, carrot, celery, leek, garlic, peppercorns, bay leaves, parsley, and thyme. Bring to a gentle simmer over medium heat, then simmer, partially covered, for 45 minutes. Strain through a colander. Refrigerate for up to 3 days, or freeze for up to 3 months.

Red Wine Syrup

MAKES ABOUT 1 CUP

6 cups red wine (two 750 mL bottles)
1 cup granulated sugar
4 bay leaves
12 whole cloves (optional)
4 whole star anise (optional)

In a large heavy saucepan, stir together wine, sugar, and bay leaves, and cloves and star anise, if using. Bring to a boil over high heat. Reduce heat to medium-high, then boil for about 1 hour, stirring occasionally, until liquid reduces to about 1 cup and becomes thick and syrupy. Strain through a fine sieve. Let cool completely. Refrigerate, covered. Keeps for up to 1 month.

Balsamic Syrup

MAKES ABOUT 1 CUP

6 cups balsamic vinegar
1⅓ cups granulated sugar

In a large heavy saucepan, stir together balsamic vinegar and sugar. Bring to a boil over high heat. Reduce heat to medium-high, then boil for about 1 hour, stirring occasionally, until liquid reduces to about 1 cup and becomes thick and syrupy. Strain through a fine sieve. Let cool completely. Refrigerate, covered. Keeps for up to 1 month.

Roasted Garlic Purée

MAKES ABOUT ½ CUP

4 whole heads garlic
4 Tbsp olive oil

Preheat the oven to 400°F. Remove any loose skin from garlic. Slice off the top third of the heads. Put garlic heads on a large square of foil. Drizzle each with 1 Tbsp oil. Wrap garlic in foil. Roast for 35–45 minutes until softened. Let cool. Pop garlic cloves from skin, then mash until smooth.

Roasted Peppers

MAKES 2 ROASTED PEPPERS

2 sweet red peppers
1 Tbsp olive oil
Salt and freshly ground black pepper

Preheat the oven to 375°F. In a large bowl, toss peppers with olive oil and salt and pepper to taste. Put peppers on a large baking sheet. Roast, turning often, for about 40 minutes or until peppers are almost completely blackened. When cool enough to handle, peel off skins, then remove stems, seeds, and any white membrane.

Clarified Butter

MAKES ABOUT 1 CUP

Clarified butter is butter from which impurities and milk solids have been removed. It has a higher smoke point than regular butter so works well in high-temperature cooking, such as frying.

Put about 1¼ cups butter in a shallow microwaveable dish. Microwave on high (100%) until completely melted. Do not boil. A film will form on top and white liquid will settle at the bottom. Let the butter rest for about 5 minutes in a warm spot. Skim off and discard any scum. Carefully remove clear butter (this is the clarified butter), discarding white liquid (milk solids) on bottom. Clarified butter will keep in the refrigerator for up to 1 month.

NOTE Unless otherwise stated in the recipes, the following assumptions are made about ingredients:
• Butter is unsalted
• Eggs are large
• Olive oil is extra virgin
• Parsley is Italian flat-leaf
• Kosher salt is preferred

Metric Conversion Charts

VOLUME

¼ tsp	1 mL
½ tsp	2 mL
¾ tsp	4 mL
1 tsp	5 mL
1½ tsp	7.5 mL
2 tsp	10 mL
1 Tbsp	15 mL
4 tsp	20 mL
1½ Tbsp	22.5 mL
2 Tbsp	30 mL
3 Tbsp	45 mL
¼ cup	60 mL
4 Tbsp	60 mL
5 Tbsp	75 mL
⅓ cup	80 mL
½ cup	125 mL
⅔ cup	160 mL
¾ cup	185 mL
1 cup	250 mL
1¼ cups	310 mL
1⅓ cups	330 mL
1½ cups	375 mL
2 cups	500 mL
3 cups	750 mL
4 cups	1 L
5 cups	1.25 L
6 cups	1.5 L
8 cups	2 L
16 cups	4 L

WEIGHT

1 oz	30 g
2 oz	60 g
2½ oz	70 g
3 oz	85 g
3½ oz	100 g
4 oz	115 g
¼ lb	115 g
6 oz	170 g
7 oz	200 g
8 oz	220 g
½ lb	220 g
¾ lb	340 g
12 oz	340 g
1 lb	450 g
1¼ lb	570 g
2 lb	900 g
2½ lb	1.1 kg
3 lb	1.5 kg
4 lb	1.8 kg
5 lb	2.3 kg

LENGTH

⅛ inch	3 mm
¼ inch	6 mm
½ inch	1 cm
¾ inch	2 cm
1 inch	2.5 cm
1½ inches	4 cm
2 inches	5 cm
3 inches	8 cm
4 inches	10 cm
5 inches	12 cm
6 inches	15 cm
7 inches	18 cm
8 inches	20 cm
9 inches	23 cm
10 inches	25 cm
11 inches	28 cm
12 inches	30 cm

TEMPERATURE

120°F	50°C
130°F	55°C
135°F	57°C
140°F	60°C
145°F	63°C
160°F	71°C
235°F	113°C
250°F	120°C
265°F	130°C
275°F	140°C
300°F	150°C
325°F	160°C
350°F	180°C
375°F	190°C
400°F	200°C
425°F	220°C
450°F	230°C

CAN SIZES

5½ oz	156 mL
14 oz	398 mL

PAN AND DISH SIZES

13- × 9-inch casserole dish/baking pan	33 × 23 cm (3.5 L) casserole dish/baking pan
9-inch round springform pan	23 cm round (2.5 L) springform pan
9- × 5-inch loaf pan	23 × 12 cm (2 L) loaf pan
8- × 4-inch loaf pan	20 × 10 cm (1.5 L) loaf pan

Acknowledgements

This cookbook started with Steve Kuijt, general manager of Island Lake Lodge, sitting down in my office and saying, "I have an idea." His idea morphed like a kid's transformer toy, and evolved into this book. Along the way, numerous people pushed, cajoled and guided, which made this volume possible. Above all, the guidance and patience of Robert McCullough and Taryn Boyd at Whitecap Books kept me going. Mauve Pagé created a look and feel fully appreciative of the Lodge's character.

At the Lodge, the chefs' contributions cannot be minimized. Thanks to Kelly Attwells, Keith Farkas, Yan Thereian, Alain Stahl, Johanne Ratthe, Kerri Maier, Mark Butcher, and Andy "Fireball" Robidoux for sharing their recipes. And an extra thanks to Keith Farkas, Fireball and Butcher for testing the recipes and adapting so many to serve just four or six, rather than the 36 they are so accustomed to serving. The recipe testing and most of Henry Georgi's food shots were staged in Christa Moffat's kitchen. For a month, Henry and Christa made every afternoon a joy. The impact of the photos falls fully in their lap.

As we put the book to bed, the final touches on the recipes came from the new Head Chef, Joe Tanti. His advice and understanding of the Lodge dining tradition assures me what passed before, carries on.

And last, as always, my thanks to Bob Mecoy for his tireless support over the years.